Memoirs of the Devil

Memoirs of the Devil

Roger Vadim

Translated by Peter Beglan
by arrangement with E.L.B.
Languages Group Ltd

Hutchinson of London

Hutchinson & Co (Publishers) Ltd
3 Fitzroy Square, London W1

London Melbourne Sydney Auckland
Wellington Johannesburg and agencies
throughout the world

© Memoirs du Diable, Editions Stock, 1975
© English translation, Hutchinson 1976

The Gamma, Sygma and Magnum photographs in this
book were supplied by the John Hillelson Agency

Set in Monotype Times

Printed in Great Britain by The Anchor Press Ltd
and bound by Wm Brendon & Son Ltd
both of Tiptree, Essex

ISBN 0 09 127670 5

Contents

Illustrations

1. Introducing the Devil

The words 'The End' came up on the screen and someone switched on the lights. The president of the board of film censors rose to his feet.

'He's the Devil!' he exclaimed.

'This film will never be shown,' declared the families' representative.

The board had been viewing a film, . . . *And Woman Was Created*, whose original French title, . . . *Et Dieu créa la femme*, with its reference to God's work, was beginning to look singularly inappropriate.

The credits showed the names of a new director, Roger Vadim, and a starlet better known for her regular appearances in glossy magazine close-ups than for mentions in film reviews.

The censors, with more insight than they are credited for, realized that the film was ushering in a new era and that cries of indignation and the wielding of scissors would be to no avail. They preferred to have nothing to do with it.

But it would have been difficult to ban it. The film's insolence and amorality lay outside the scope of the law. Despite one or two cuts (which would make a schoolgirl smile indulgently today) Brigitte Bardot was delivered unveiled and free of bourgeois taboos to the public. She was to cross national borders to give the world a foretaste of a new morality. In her inimitably shameless manner she flouted the Ten Commandments by demonstrating that sex was no longer a sin. There was nothing diabolical about this explosion of pagan candour, but something had been started: the posters proclaimed that

'Woman was created by God and BB was invented by the Devil'. The nickname has stuck to me ever since.

I was the Devil to all the censors who ever had to view my films. But I was also the Devil to mothers, representatives of the Church – and, because it made good copy, to journalists as well. I earned myself the title of the Devil by creating and portraying beauty, by transforming innocent young girls into two-dimensional goddesses. A Devil with Bluebeard tendencies, marrying and divorcing them into the bargain. Although divorce was a well-established part of our way of life, it was as though I had given it its letters patent, writ in sulphur. I also, apparently, ran my sports cars and motor boat on sulphur.

Does he exist, this Devil of the cinema, this Devil conjured up so frequently by the journalists? In all modesty, I doubt it.

But who knows?

If it were true, it would be flattering.

2. In praise of kidnappers – and teeth

My first memory is of a vast white carpet. Someone is holding my hand. I want to let go and walk unaided. The temptation is all the greater since I can make holes in the snow when I walk. . . . I once described the spot to my mother. She replied that it was a garden in Warsaw where I took my first steps and that I couldn't possibly remember it because I was only ten months old at the time. It seems it's impossible to have such clear memories of being ten months old. I am quite happy to accept this, but if it isn't a memory, what is it?

I do not have many memories of my childhood: for instance, the voice of my father, Igor Plémiannikov, but not his face . . .

Fourteen months. My paternal grandparents' little flat in Warsaw.
ME: Can I have a sweet, please?
MY FATHER: Say it in Russian.
ME: *Da mnie pajalsti karfleton.*

Alexandria, 1932–3? In the consulate courtyard. I am playing in my father's car. A white convertible with a little pointed tail, a racing car. My sister is afraid of something and I am playing with the car in much the same way as a child would play with a big dog.

Alexandria, about the same time. I am in the hall and the fat Egyptian cleaning woman is washing the stairs. The front door opens. My father appears. The cleaning woman turns round and screams. For a Muslim woman it is an act of gross indecency to show her face to a man. In her panic she snatches up her skirts to cover her face, affording a generous view of her buttocks and belly. With her skirts still held aloft, she turns round and rushes up the stairs. I hear my father laugh, but I'm puzzled: 'How can a woman show a stranger her bottom, but not her face . . . ?' At the age of five I had just discovered that the rules of decency, as applied to the feminine body, were rather variable – they seemed to depend on geographical location and religion.

Alexandria, same period. I am walking back to the consulate with my governess and my sister. We are walking uphill. I hear a cry. A man is pinned against the front door in a curious position. Head hanging down, arms open, the palms of his hands nailed to the heavy wooden door. Crucified. The governess hides her face in her hands. There was a lot of nationalist feeling in the air and Europeans were being nailed to doors from time to time.

Shortly after this incident the grocer's delivery boy caught the plague and one of our playmates dropped dead with cerebro-spinal meningitis in our drawing-room; my mother rushed back to France with my sister and me. Meanwhile my father was posted to Turkey. First to Samsun on the Black Sea, and then to Mersin in the south near the Syrian border.

Life in Mersin was fun. Every two or three weeks there was a hanging in the market-place. The condemned men were dressed in long white shifts pinned to which were lists of their crimes. After execution their bodies were left to dangle in the breeze all morning. On hanging days I always used to accompany the cook when she went to do the shopping; my mother was delighted that a little boy of seven should be so eager to help.

Being kidnapped was even more exciting. One morning we were being driven in an *araba* (a sort of open carriage) to the beach when a man jumped up beside the driver. After unceremoniously inviting the governess and the

driver to get out, he whipped up the horse and drove my
sister and me off to an unknown destination. The object
of the exercise was not to obtain a ransom but to draw
attention to the local Turks' disapproval of French policy
towards Syria. Our abductors took us to a rather poor
house occupied by a couple and their five children. We
were given the parents' bedroom, the only one where
there was a real bed. They slept outside the door on a
pallet. Luckily, the Turks adore children: once a year, on
children's day, kids are allowed to do whatever they want
from dusk to dawn. Hélène and I were in ecstasy. Our
every whim was pandered to, we were stuffed with Turkish
Delight, halva and sweets. But all good things, alas, come
to an end. A compromise was found and we had to go
home.

Despite our secret hopes, there were no more kid-
nappings. Life was in danger of relapsing into the humdrum
when, just in time, the mass grave turned up. Several
thousand French soldiers had been killed in some obscure
and pointless battle which had taken place in the area in
1917. They had all been buried together in a communal
grave and my father was given the job of supervising the
repatriation of their remains.

The bones had to be arranged according to type – tibia
with tibia, humerus with humerus, patella with patella,
and so on, and returned to France, where, I suppose,
they would be shared out equitably among the dead
heroes' relations. Pending their glorious return by ship to
the mother country, our proud warriors were lined up on
the ground floor of the consulate in potato sacks. I was
fascinated by this treasury of skulls, finger-joints, ribs and
collar-bones. 'Those generals must have had a whale of a
time,' I thought to myself.

At the time I was losing my milk teeth and on at least
two occasions my mother gave me a present after looking
under my pillow and finding a canine which had belonged
to some poor soldier. I also stole a magnificent molar with

which I used to tease Marcelle, the secretary's daughter. Marcelle, who was nine and in love with me, used to lie in wait in the garden or in some deserted room, hoping for a chance to give me a kiss. I would brandish the molar under her nose, and she would run off screaming with me in hot pursuit, shouting: 'The tooth! The tooth!' Four years later she still used to burst into tears if she saw a boy who looked like me in the street, or so her father told us in a letter.

3. Treasure

I was a healthy, gifted child – seven years old and without a care in the world. My parents loved each other and loved me. Although we had no money, we lived like millionaires. But God is watching over us and knows what He is doing. I was going to pay for all the unearned happiness I had enjoyed since the cradle.

It was July 1937, not the fourteenth, but a holiday all the same. A holiday brought to perfection by the pure mountain air of Savoie, by the fat yellow sun and the clear blue sky, by the crystal-clear light playing on the dining-room wallpaper with its pattern of flowers and birds. It was a holiday because my father, who was so young and so kind, was on leave and having breakfast with his wife and children.

When he slumped forward, his face falling into his bowl of coffee, my sister burst out laughing. But I knew from the very first instant. I knew it was over. That death was not only the sheet-white face of my father, who would be gone by the next day, but an obscene intruder who determines the course of people's lives. In that instant I aged more than I have ever aged since. It was not that my father no longer existed, but that a grotesque, faceless monster had taken his place. A monster which would never go away.

My father had only fainted; he was to die twenty-four hours later. My sister's laugh changed into an animal howl, an unending monotone. I didn't want to cry out – I knew that it wouldn't change anything and that, if he'd been able to hear, it would have upset my father. But that horrible, uncontrolled screaming was contagious. I resisted with all my strength. I said to myself: 'It's not civilized, I can't scream like that.' And then, suddenly, it came up from the gut, like a fit of vomiting. My voice mingled with my sister's in a cry of primeval suffering.

From that day on we had to live on a third of the wages of a post-office clerk – my mother's pension (my father had forgotten to pay the last instalment on his life insurance). However, I have no memory of being affected in any way by the change from privileged life to one of total penury. In fact, my mind is a virtual blank when I try to relive the two years following my father's death. The mobilization, the phoney war, journeys by road and in packed trains, the 1940 armistice: these are things I only remember vicariously through other people's experiences. But one incident still remains vivid, even after all these years.

We had taken refuge in my godmother's house in Alès and my mother had managed to find a job in a chemicals factory. Unfortunately for us, however, my godmother's husband was an ardent supporter of Pétain and quickly became alarmed by my mother's avowedly Communist loyalties. Terrified of being compromised, our host reported her to the local police.

By selling our last Persian carpet to the manager of the chemicals factory we managed to raise enough money to escape. We ended up under the sun and pine trees of Minelle, near Mandelieu-La Napoule, a dozen kilometres outside Cannes. It was a dreamland with only one drawback – there was nothing to eat. My sister and I worked for a farmer picking and packing peaches. For two months our diet consisted entirely of peaches, pine seeds and grape sugar – morning, noon and evening. Then one day we received a letter from our aunt, the heiress. This aunt claimed to be a princess and, according to family tradition, she had fled from Russia with a fortune in jewellery and precious stones. 'Come,' said the letter, 'since my attack, I have become a cripple. You are the only people I wish to leave my Treasure to.'

Our aunt the heiress lived in Tourette-Levens, forty kilometres to the north of Nice. We had just enough money to pay for two single bus fares – naturally, we had no worries about the return journey, since we would undoubtedly be rich by then. After twenty-four hours of dreaming about our new life as millionaires my mother and I caught the bus, while Hélène, my little sister, jumped up and down on the roadside waving goodbye like a lunatic.

Our miserly aunt lived with her hidden Treasure in an old château some three kilometres outside the village. As we walked there, we practised putting on serious faces to hide our glee.

The château came into view at the last turn in the road. Or, more exactly, what remained of the château. It was in ruins, with only one wing still standing. This worried me, but my mother reminded me that rich misers always starved to death on mattresses stuffed with banknotes. The idea of adding discomfort to starvation struck me as being uncivilized, but I refrained from commenting.

We found our aunt the heiress in a damp room which stank of stale milk and urine. She got up from her armchair squealing like a squirrel, supporting herself on two ivory-handled walking sticks. She looked genuinely old and decrepit, but I didn't particularly like her habit of suddenly raising an arm in the middle of a conversation and waving one of her sticks in the air. For a dying woman she seemed to have plenty of energy.

After rambling on for two hours or more about her property in the Ukraine and her late husband, the Prince, she finally led us – with our patience at breaking point – into another room. An interesting-looking chest was plainly visible, standing on top of a sideboard.

'You are going to see something extraordinary,' announced my aunt. And, with a loving gesture, she lifted the lid. I have never been so close to a fortune. And I have never hated a man so much. I can still hear his name:

General Borowski. He had massacred three thousand Bolsheviks in a single day, but as far as I was concerned his real crime was that he, in effigy, was the sole occupant of the chest. Goodbye rubies, goodbye jewels, goodbye fortune. Borowski – who had no doubt had his fun with the old girl in 1918 – had been killed getting her across the Polish border and she had venerated him like a saint ever since. Piously she kissed the yellowing photograph and returned it to the chest.

'And where is the treasure?' I asked, giving up all pretence at diplomacy.

'Follow me,' she said.

Off we went, hopes still high, following the old lady as she tottered along on her sticks. We came to a halt between two olive trees in a close-cropped field, at a respectful distance from the horns of a nanny goat which seemed to hold us responsible for the meagreness of its diet.

'Good morning, Treasure,' said the aunt fondly to her goat.

Treasure was bad-tempered. Even our aunt the heiress approached her with circumspection. Relations between the two of them were tense, but this did not preclude love, and the little old lady, who was due to go into a home three days later, didn't want to sell her or leave her to the 'barbarians' – as she called her neighbours. With the fortune forgotten, I saw the Princess in a different light. A very lonely, very old lady, who lived in the distant past and was going to end her days playing at make-believe, a naughty child among other naughty children as old as herself. In a home. And the intruder, the monster, death, allowed her to totter on.

From Tourette-Levens to Mandelieu-La Napoule was a distance of ninety kilometres; we had no money and, to make matters worse, we were encumbered with our inheritance. We set out on foot. Treasure was in a bad mood and used my backside for target practice. As fatigue set in, she seemed to become reconciled to the human race and, by sunset, we had become companions in distress.

We spent the first night in a barn. By the morning, Treasure had adopted me and taken to licking instead of butting me.

Hitch-hiking with a goat isn't easy, but we were lucky – a lorry with a load of cement took pity on us. Keeping your balance on a pile of sacks with a terrified goat isn't easy either, but, as my grandmother used to say, 'you have to take the rough with the smooth'. That evening, we arrived at the railway station of Saint-Martin-du-Var. Treasure was exhausted, her udders fit to burst, and I had no idea how to set about milking her. However, the station-master was a kindly man and after my mother, who was not without charm, had read his palm, he showed me how to milk the poor animal and put us up in a shed containing furniture which was bound for Germany. He particularly recommended a bed in which Napoléon had slept after his escape from Elba, and which was now on its way to Marshal Goering's country house. Treasure's friendship had by now developed into a passion and she spent the night sleeping at my feet on the bed.

The next morning the worthy station-master put Treasure, my mother and me on to a goods wagon and we got as far as Grasse without further difficulty.

We travelled the remainder of the journey on foot. The weather was fine and we had milk. We sang out of tune, but our hearts were in unison. Our dreams had been shattered, but we still had our happiness.

Her name was Marcelle, the same as my little friend from Mersin.

Her father and mother had been murdered, practically before her eyes, by a gang of young thugs. She was eleven years old. An orphan overnight, she had left Nice and I met her at the village school in Minelle. Although I was a year older than her, I was much more shy and she kissed me on the beach at La Napoule, throwing her arms around my neck between two waves and pressing her lips to my mouth as though by accident. First kisses, all salty, scarcely felt before they were washed away – and I like a mug pretended not to notice.

She wrote I L—V— Y—U in the sand, asking me to fill in the blanks – and I like a mug pretended not to understand. So she filled in the missing letters.

She never talked about her parents. We used to steal lilies from the school garden. We would leave our bicycles behind the trees and she would ask me to kiss her. And I like a mug kissed her on the cheeks.

My mother didn't want me to see her. She thought that Marcelle was a bad influence on me. At the slightest sign of emotion or happiness, parents always say: 'He (or she) is a bad influence on you.' This upsets and confuses children. It spoils their happiness. I promised myself that I would never fall into this trap if I had children one day. Alas, I fear that I have not lived up to my promise.

So, Marcelle was a bad influence on me. From then on I saw her in secret, but, despite what people say, the fact that our relationship was a clandestine one added nothing to my happiness. It has never given me any pleasure to deceive a woman, either my mother or, later on, a wife. So, with no great enthusiasm, I used to meet Marcelle secretly on the hillside. One day she lay down and threatened to take her knickers off. My courage failed me. Marcelle waited. I waited. The interminable silence became too much for her patience. She undid, or rather tore off, her blouse. She snatched at an arbutus tree, grabbing handfuls of the red berries and pressing them to the nascent buds of her breasts. The juice looked like blood staining her skin. I could find nothing to say. Nothing to do. I could not even look. I simply understood. Then, with a sort of suppressed rage, without haste and without ostentation, she undressed. She took everything off. Her skirt, her knickers, her shoes and her socks. Even the vaccination dressing on her arm. I didn't dare to look at that hairless bulging cleft about which I had been fantasizing at the slightest provocation, night or day – even during classes.

She lay on her back, stones and dead twigs clinging to her skin. She felt a little stupid and so did I. She thought I was afraid of the arbutus blood on her breasts, or perhaps of her thrashing open legs. In fact, I was afraid of being unable to find a plausible lie. It was only at night that I loved Marcelle and she excited me. Not when I saw her. But how could I tell her that?

Marcelle got up. She grabbed some more berries, knocking most of them to the ground and covered her stomach with their juice. Prickly though they were, she pushed them between her thighs. It looked as though everything was going inside her. But it was like crushing strawberries against a window-pane. She lost her temper and it all squirted out. 'You're afraid, you're afraid,' she screamed. 'You're afraid of blood!' She stood bolt upright, completely naked and red all over.

I couldn't help remembering the murder, the dreadful event which she never mentioned. I saw the mother, a woman of film-star beauty, in a pale yellow nightdress stained with her own blood, and the father, ugly, overweight, the opposite of my father, his head turned away to avoid seeing what was happening.

While this nightmare was flashing through my mind, I stayed very calm – almost lazy, as if I was lying in the sun on a beach mattress.

Treasure had followed us and was now gazing curiously at the extraordinary scene in front of her. I stumbled, grabbed her right horn and walked down the hillside.

Marcelle never came back to school.

4. Freud's loss, my gain

20 November 1942. The noise of thunder woke me up; it wasn't yet day. Dardenne, where we lived among the vineyards, overlooked Toulon, which was about five kilometres away as the crow flies. From a first-floor window, we watched a false dawn rising from the sea, a red and purple dawn. These weren't the colours of the sun, but of warfare.

'The Americans are landing!' yelled my overjoyed sister.

'The Americans!' echoed my mother.

Later, we learnt from the wireless that the Germans had broken the armistice agreement and invaded the free zone. The French fleet was scuttling itself, and disappearing into the silence of the water.

Then the ammunition dumps exploded. The oil-storage tanks blazed like gigantic torches, twisting in slow, sensual convulsions.

At ten o'clock I decided to go and have a look. While my mother was busy with my sister in the kitchen, I slipped out. The trams weren't running, so I took my bicycle.

At the entrance to the town I was suddenly engulfed in darkness. Everything was covered by an impenetrable shroud of black smoke from the blazing oil, which went on burning for two days. The only light in Toulon came from spasmodic explosions and from German military vehicles driving around the town with their headlamps full on.

Trucks loaded with soldiers – looking like insects with forty heads and phosphorescent eyes – artillery, armoured cars, motor-bikes with and without sidecars and tanks, tanks, tanks. . . . The procession went on and on. I now know that it was only a single division, a minor component of the great Nazi machine. But in the midst of that man-made night, with its mad colour scheme of red and black, I felt I was in the presence of a supernatural, invincible force, a strikingly beautiful snake of steel, a hateless and heartless visitor from another world.

In the boulevard de Strasbourg I left my bike and crossed the snake, which had at last come to a standstill. I went down towards the port, where there wasn't much fighting going on. The sailors were surrendering quietly and letting the Germans go on board their ships. To begin with, the soldiers were getting themselves blown up as the charges detonated, but, learning quickly from experience, they gave up venturing aboard and settled for marching the disarmed sailors off towards the munitions factory. A few lifeless bodies littered the narrow streets, scattered here and there by some sadistic, parsimonious giant. A week earlier I had seen the body of an electrocuted workman and been deeply distressed. Now, at the sight of war victims, I felt nothing at all. Later in life I found that this selective reaction to death was part of my make-up. A corpse at the scene of a road accident can upset me more than the sight of an entire family lying in the rubble of their bombed-out home.

Then I saw the girl. The 12A, the Seyne tram, was turned over on its side and she was lying on the rear wheel, her head flung back in profile against the dirty black steel, her legs splayed at an unnatural angle. I no longer remember whether she was wearing a school smock or a skirt, but she was naked from the waist down. I guessed she was twelve years old, probably because 12A was the number of the tram. She was as white as a sheet, as dead people generally are. And very beautiful. But of course in that deceptive hell of troubled darkness and ceaseless thunder my imagination could have been playing tricks with me. The cobbled streets shook under the weight of the tanks and, from time to time, the girl's body shuddered.

I was in love with that girl for years. I was convinced that had she not been killed she would have loved me. In my day-dreams I imagined her sleeping beside me, kissing me, walking with me through the pine forests, resting her head on my shoulder as we sat together on a night train which never reached its destination.

I gave her a name: Sophie.

The sailors taken prisoner after the scuttling of the fleet were being held inside the perimeter of the munitions factory. I knew about ten of them well, as they had spent Christmas with us (they lived in the occupied zone and were taken in by local families when they couldn't spend their leave at home). I had spotted a partly demolished house near the wall of the munitions factory area. I was able to get in through a hole. Once inside, I walked up to the German soldier on guard and asked to speak to one of the prisoners, giving his name and saying that he was my brother. He was brought out, we chatted and, as we did so, moved gradually out of the sentry's line of vision. Then I guided my friend to the hole and liberty. The method seemed to involve so little risk that I used it again the next day. This time I asked to speak to my uncle and was quickly granted permission. The Toulon sailors had not joined forces with the Allies and were not really looked upon as enemies. Nevertheless they had fought after their fashion and were being kept prisoners until the Germans decided what to do with them.

The third time round I was unlucky enough to hit on the same sentry as on the first day. He came to the conclusion that I had rather too many relations in the navy and asked to see my pass. By the time he had brought his rifle up to his shoulder, I was fifty yards away. I heard him shout 'Halt!' once or twice and then there was a shot.

B

Perhaps he fired into the air because of my short trousers. Or perhaps he was just a bad shot.

During those three visits I had picked up a couple of dozen unfired machine-gun bullets. Instead of doing my algebra I amused myself by pulling the bullets out of their cases to get at the powder. My scheme was to run a trail of powder as far as my desk and then to light it at the psychological moment. The first part of the exercise succeeded beyond my wildest dreams. A superb trail of fire and smoke flashed across the classroom. The nervous chemistry master, on edge after the morning's air-raid warning, was already streaking down the corridor when the roar of laughter told him the truth.

The chemistry master may not have been a courageous man, but he was vindictive. I was had up before the disciplinary board and expelled – which was bad luck for me since I had already been sacked from the school on the other side of the street three months earlier. On that occasion we had been set the task of illustrating the Marshal's motto: 'Work, Family, Country', and the best drawings were to be displayed in the school hall for the edification of the school inspector. Adopting a satirical style, I had depicted a family polishing a German officer's boots, while the Marshal rolled out a carpet whose shape was clearly reminiscent of France minus Alsace and Lorraine. I had pinned my masterpiece up in the school hall myself.

However, the inspector had not found it to his taste.

My mother decided that we would go and live in the Alps again where I would continue my studies by correspondence. Since I had taken so badly to the reactionary discipline of school, it was up to me to prove that I could do better without blinkers and the big stick.

My mother rented a large farmhouse near the Col des Gets at a peppercorn rent. Today the Col des Gets is a fairly well-known ski resort. In 1943 it was a village with a population of 980 and had only a little mechanical ski-lift. From it, a mule track wound its way up to the hamlet of Les Folliets, a distance of about four kilometres. The hamlet, which was cut off from the village whenever there was a heavy fall of snow, consisted of three farmhouses, built in the purest Savoie style, with shingle roofs, stables separated from the living quarters by a corridor and granaries on the first floor. The last of these was our new home. We pumped our water into a trough (a hollowed-out tree-trunk outside the front door) and in winter we had to break off the icicle which materialized each night. We had oil lamps for light and did our cooking on the huge stove in the living-room. Naturally there was no telephone.

Before long, my mother met and fell in love with Gérald Hanning, an architect who was the first wanted man to find sanctuary in our farmhouse. At the time of the armistice he had been arrested trying to get across the Spanish border and imprisoned in the fort at Ha, in Bordeaux. He had escaped, and his mother (a friend of my mother) had sent him to us. Love knows no prejudice and Gérald's gratitude to Propi (as my mother was nicknamed) soon developed into love, despite the difference in their ages. He was fifteen years younger than her, but I spared Propi the soul-searching which mothers usually suffer under such circumstances (my poor boy! to see his mummy in the arms of a young man! jealousy! trauma! insecurity!). I took the most benevolent view possible of this romance and gave them every encouragement. I was delighted. Freud's loss, my gain.

5. Anouk Aimée

Pupu was the official guide in the area. A smuggler by profession, the war had converted him into a hero of the Resistance. For a reasonable pecuniary consideration he would guide Jews, Communists or anyone who was in serious trouble with the Gestapo or Pétain's police over the border to Switzerland. I know several people whom he saved from the firing squad or the concentration camp.

Unfortunately, Pupu's morale crumbled at the slightest domestic scene. After a row with his wife he would shut himself up and brood in solitude for days on end. Any callers would be referred to me, since I knew the route to the border and the habits of the German patrols, having accompanied him on several of his expeditions.

One evening in the winter of 1943-4 a horse-drawn sleigh drew up outside our door at dinner-time. When I went out to investigate I found a man of about forty who seemed to be in a high state of nerves. He told me that Pupu had sent him. He was Jewish and wanted to get to Switzerland immediately. I remember only that he had a limp and that his first name was Georges.

Even in fine weather it took a day to reach the Col de Cou, which was the nearest point at which one could cross into Switzerland. In falling snow, and with a lame and inexperienced skier for companion, it was well-nigh impossible. We had to wait for a break in the weather.

During the forty-eight hours he spent at the farmhouse Georges spoke a lot about someone he had met a few days previously in Megève – a young actor who had made a big impression on him.

However, during the journey to the border, Georges

was too busy to open his mouth – with his skis weighed down by sealskins, he had difficulty in keeping up with me in the powdery snow. We reached the Col de Cou before nightfall. The German patrol always passed at around midday, since the chalet where they spent the night was several hours away. The Col was shrouded in low cloud. We were already in Switzerland when there was a strident call of 'Halt!' followed by the crackle of rifle fire. Had the Germans lost their way in the mist and fallen behind schedule? Or were they new to the job? As they were firing into Swiss territory, the second possibility seemed more likely. But it was no time for conjecture and I made myself scarce, slaloming as I went. I hoped they would not dare cross the border.

The firing stopped and I heard the Germans talking among themselves. I turned and saw Georges lying prostrate in the snow. I went back. He was hurt in the leg, but didn't know whether he had broken it or been shot in the knee. I took off his skis and was trying to lift him on to my back when two soldiers suddenly broke away from the patrol and came racing towards us.

Quickly, I asked Georges to give me the notebook in which he had written down my address. (He had promised to send me some milk powder and chocolate from Switzerland.) There was nothing more that I could do for him and I abandoned him to his sinister fate.

While I was staying with a Swiss peasant family waiting for things to blow over, I opened the notebook and, inside, found a photograph which had been cut out of a newspaper and folded in four. It was a picture of the young actor who had made such a strong impression on Georges.

Five years later I was having dinner in a Montparnasse restaurant with Gérard Philipe and asked him if he had met a man of about forty in a Megève hotel in January or February 1944, who had a limp and liked to talk theatre. I tried to describe Georges to him. After a few moments' thought Gérard Philipe confirmed that he did indeed remember such a man. And he smiled . . . I think he liked the stranger things in life and considered them perfectly natural.

At that time I was going to the private school run by M. and Mme Rossi in Morzine. It meant a considerable journey every day. In summer I went on foot and by bicycle. In winter, I went on skis, by road or, whenever it was working, by the Le Planay cable car. But it was at the Rossi's school that I met the most charming of little girls – eleven, romantic, intelligent and subtly cruel. A perfect creature. I was in love with her from the very first second. Unfortunately, I was not alone. My feelings were shared by every other boy in the class, about ten of them altogether. The girl of our dreams had a rather ordinary name: Françoise Durand. But it was a wartime name, as her father was of Jewish extraction. She was to become known later under the stage name of Anouk Aimée.

I arrived at the Rossi establishment for the first time one afternoon and was introduced to the other pupils. It was the period for doing homework and the headmaster left the room. I found myself sitting next to this wondrous creature and suddenly my heart stopped beating. In the grip of an uncontrollable surge of amorous feeling I took it upon myself to run through my impressions of Jerry Lewis. I stuck my fingers in the inkwell, dribbled, made half a dozen attempts at picking up my book, giggled like a caveman who has just invented the wheel, tried to pick my nose but poked myself in the eye instead, and so on. In other words, I went through the complete repertoire of the sophisticated charmer.

The next day Anouk Aimée's aunt asked to see M. Rossi and, with some embarrassment, explained that she respected him for taking on handicapped children, but that her niece had had nightmares all night, so she would appreciate it if we could be put into different classes.

Once the misunderstanding had been cleared up, things

began to go better for me. It took an hour for me to reduce the other boys' six months of work to nothing. I became the favourite, the chosen one, and that is how it stayed.

If this platonic love never developed into a grand passion, it was only because of a cruel twist of fate. Or, more precisely, a chamber-pot. We were playing hide-and-seek in a friend's house one day when I found myself with Anouk in the promising darkness of a cupboard. It seemed as if nothing could prevent the inevitable from happening: our destinies were about to become entwined for ever. Suddenly she burst out laughing. It was a long, lilting laugh which I remember to this day. I had not noticed that I was sitting on a chamber-pot. And I had imagined it was a cloud.

It was during this period that I decided to play Cupid between my mother and Popa Gérald Hanning. I wanted them to get married. My motives were not so much moral or religious as practical. Our beloved Marshal, bent on increasing the population, was handing out footwear coupons to couples who got married – and my ambition was to possess a pair of ski boots made of real leather.

A few forms to fill in, a promise to the Mayor, wasn't that a small price for our generous parents to pay? After a month's persistence I reaped my reward. I didn't attend the wedding, which took place on 12 December 1943 in the town hall at Gets. Instead, I treated myself to an excellent morning's skiing. I turned up at school in the afternoon with a cast-iron excuse for missing the morning classes: 'Sir, I didn't come to school this morning because my mummy got married.' It was rejected out of hand and I got two hours' detention. Only Anouk Aimée realized intuitively that I was telling the truth and suggested to M. Rossi that he put off my punishment until the next day to give me an opportunity of proving that the marriage had taken place.

With my new boots I improved my skiing tremendously.

There are no secrets in village life. The local gendarmes –
who had no direct link with Pétain's militia, but sometimes had to carry out arrests – let my mother know that
it would be prudent to get as far away as possible from the
Col des Gets. We decided to go to Paris by way of Grenoble.

There were dangers involved in staying in Grenoble.
My sister and I were fourteen and fifteen years old, but
Baby Gullu, my foster-brother, was scarcely eight. My
mother thought it more sensible to put him into a convent
in Annecy for a week. We were to pick him up on the way
back.

Baby Gullu, alias Jessie Plémiannikov, had been born
in Samsun, Turkey, on the Black Sea, the love-child of
the French consulate's young Turkish cook and the
American representative of Chesterfield cigarettes. Miss
Gullu, who had heard the Americans call everything in
nappies 'baby', had assumed that it was a name and had
her child christened accordingly. However, the father,
who was a respectable man with a wife in Washington,
had shown no desire to have anything to do with any
baby, let alone Baby. Miss Gullu found consolation in the
arms of the *kavass* (chauffeur-cum-secretary-cum-door-
man), a man of character, but hardly enthusiastic about
taking on a family. He had decided to take off with the
young cook, who abandoned the three-week-old Baby
Gullu on the consulate porch. My mother inherited the
little bundle, who was rechristened Jessie and brought up
as the third child of the family. Baby Gullu/Jessie was a
dark-skinned, thick-set little boy with a hooked nose –
stubborn, untruthful, a little scatological and nobody's
fool.

In Grenoble friends hid us for a day and a night and
then drove us to Lyons where we managed to get a train
to Paris. Given the circumstances, there could be no
question of stopping off at Annecy to pick up Baby Gullu.
As he was safe with the nuns, my mother decided that she
would come back to collect him when we had settled in

the capital and she would be able to make the journey without risk.

Thanks to Le Corbusier, a friend of Gérald's, we set up home in the place du Dr Blanche (near the avenue Mozart) in a magnificent villa built in 1930 and previously occupied by a family of Swedes who had left at the beginning of the war. The days went by and we received no answers to our letters from the nuns at Annecy. At first we blamed the vagaries of the wartime post, but after a month my mother bought a ticket to Annecy. That same day we received a letter from Baby Gullu: 'Dear Mme Plémiannikov, I am well. Mother Emmanuelle and Sister Clotilde are very pleased with me. Father Simon is very proud of my progress in catechism. I hope you are all well in Paris. Please give my regards to Vadim and his sister Hélène. Thank you for everything. Jean-Marc.'

Why was the silly idiot sending me his regards and writing 'Dear Mme Plémiannikov' to Propi? I was furious, although it was obvious that the letter had been dictated to him. And why Jean-Marc? What was wrong with Baby Gullu or Jessie? The next day a letter containing all the answers arrived from the Mother Superior.

The good sisters had apparently been moved to compassion by this little boy who had been born a Muslim and was, in consequence, an infidel condemned to eternal fire. In the best traditions of the crusades they had decided to save his soul. As he had not been adopted legally by my mother (and could not be), they had baptized him Jean-Marc according to Catholic ritual and set about finding him foster-parents. A pious and no doubt worthy couple, M. and Mme Cosette, grocers living in a village thirty kilometres from Annecy, met the statutory criteria (over forty-five, no living children, good reputation, etc.) and Baby Gullu, alias Jessie Plémiannikov, duly became Jean-Marc Cosette.

My mother had no recourse under the law. Kidnap him? An unpromising solution even in peacetime; under the Occupation it was out of the question. Sentimental blackmail? An unintelligent weapon and one which would achieve nothing. We took the sickening decision to accept the inevitable and abandon him to his new parents. They were in all probability kind people who would do everything to make him happy. Besides, Baby Gullu was not too well suited to the bohemian way of life. He was a creature of habit. We wished him well.

I secretly wrote to him telling him that if things turned out badly he could always run away and find refuge with us, but that, all things considered (food being one of his main interests in life), there was a great deal to be said for becoming a grocer. The letter presumably never reached him. I have often thought of visiting him in his village, but so far have always thought better of it. If Jean-Marc Cosette is still alive and happens to read this book, I would like him to know that I should be delighted to drink a cup of tea with him one day.

6. Paris

Paris welcomed me: the gates to the overhead Métro all bore my initials, V.P. There they stood for Ville de Paris, but elsewhere, chalked up on the walls of the city, they stood for '*Vive Pétain*', the answer to other daubers' V for victory.

The clichés about the period are fairly true. The Germans. The curfew. The bicycle-taxis. The front-wheel-drive motor cars used by the occupying forces and the collaborators. Gas generators. Ration books. Queues. The Métro missing out every other station. Civil defence. Blacked-out windows and sandbags. Sirens. ARP. Policemen on bikes. Queues. More queues. Fiddling. Making ends meet. The black market. House raids. Occasional shootings.

But Paris was alive. One was aware of oppression, but not of submission. There was the rule of iron – the Nazis – and moral leadership in the shape of the French Government. But it was possible to reject either or both. That was freedom.

I read Mark Twain, Stendhal, Kierkegaard and Gorki, Diderot, Ilia Ehrenburg, Selma Lagerlöf and Swift, *Hope* by Malraux, Céline's *Death on the Instalment Plan* and the *Life of Lenin*.

I went to the school of oriental languages. My career had been mapped out. Political science. An entrance exam for the Foreign Service. No major problems for a diplomat's son. I found it easy to see myself as a consul, an ambassador or Foreign Minister.

But Propi saw things more clearly: she wanted me to have a choice, not just the easiest option. She knew of my penchant for the theatre and the arts. She told me about

Charles Dullin, who ran the Théâtre de la Cité and had a drama school.

On the way to the rue de Lille one morning I stopped, as much out of idleness as anything else, in the place du Châtelet. The head of Dullin's drama school, Lucien Arnaud, saw me in his office. 'Go away and learn a part,' he told me, 'and then come and see me again.' He suggested a Lafcadio monologue.

I went back. He listened. What he heard did not convince him that I was a genius, but he nevertheless advised me to take part in the auditions at which Charles Dullin would be selecting his first-year pupils. On the way out I met a thin highly-strung boy with a large nose and big eyes. He told me his name: Marcel Marceau. He was new as well and was learning a piece from *The Brothers Karamazov* for the audition.

'Guess which character?'

'Smerdyakov,' I replied.

'Yes,' answered Marceau. 'I'm too good-looking, of course, but I'll get over that somehow.'

He offered me a cup of coffee in the basement café and asked me if I found him ugly.

'As ugly as a mirror,' I answered.

Marceau, who lives permanently at a remove of several light years from the rest of us, understands things in his own way. He burst out laughing ten minutes later.

'Do you know about the school's hierarchy and how it works?' he asked.

'No.'

'You are a probationer for three months to a year. You go to the classes and take private tuition from Arnaud. Then preparatory class for one or two years. You go through scenes during the classes, generally with Arnaud. The senior class gets Dullin. He fills the minor roles at the theatre with senior-class pupils. Promotion from one grade to another is decided at the annual audition.'

'It all sounds very slow.'

'Well,' said Marceau, 'I'm going to get straight into the senior class.'

'Why?'

'Dullin is a genius. Genius must recognize genius. And I have no time to lose.'

I was not convinced that genius could recognize genius, but Marcel exuded total confidence. Taking my leave of him, I decided that I didn't have three years to lose either and that I too was going to get into the senior class.

Lafcadio's verse bored me to tears. Three days before the audition I changed my mind and learned the part of the madman in Courteline's *Le Commissaire est bon enfant*. My penchant for the absurd was destined to bear fruit.

On the morning of the audition I asked the other students if they had ever heard of probationers being taken straight into the senior class. 'No, that's never happened,' was their unanimous reply.

I took this information as an incentive. On the little workshop stage I saw Dullin for the first time – a gnarled hunchback with a pointed face. From under a lowered brow which occasionally darted upwards his eyes glinted at you: twin laser beams which made the bravest men blanch and the most seasoned troupers shake at the knees. The mouth was both thin-lipped and sensuous, seemingly full of menace even when it was smiling. He was a man possessed. Possessed by his passion for the theatre. He was King Lear and Savonarola, Richard III and Harpagon, all rolled into one. The traitor and the saint. The jealous husband and the lover. The victim and the murderer. I liked him from the first moment, and never felt afraid of him.

The results of the audition were given out the next day. Six students from the preparatory class were promoted to the senior class. Two probationers were also taken into the senior class: Marcel Marceau and myself.

To earn a little pocket money, or to pay their way

through the school, the students worked as extras in the plays put on by the Théâtre de la Cité (the name given to the Théâtre Sarah Bernhardt during the Occupation, on the orders of the Kommandantur). In *King Lear*, decked out in a shapeless sack, I was a 'figure on the heath'. More a piece of the scenery than an extra. One morning I was over an hour late for rehearsals. Dullin noticed my absence immediately.

'Very well, since one of the cast is missing,' he had exclaimed with a sweep of the arms, 'we shall wait for him!'

And the thirty-two actors and seventy extras waited. An hour went by. Dullin stalked up and down, the indignant victim of a crime of treason against the Theatre.

Eventually, hoping to sneak in unnoticed, I slipped in at the back of the stage and took up my half-concealed position among the eighteen other 'figures on the heath'.

'Ah, so we deign to attend at rehearsals!'

In the deathly silence of the immense theatre, Dullin's voice resounded like the trumpets of the last judgement.

'So we're trying to sabotage Shakespeare! Jeopardize the whole play three days before dress rehearsals, would you?'

'But, M. Dullin,' I faltered, 'I have an excuse. I am ill ...'

'And what about me? Aren't I always ill?' answered the hunchbacked genius. 'I'm always ill. But I'm here!'

Plainly a logical approach was pointless. Without thinking, I said:

'But in my case, M. Dullin, it's cholera.'

A hundred and two pairs of lungs held their breath: their owners were expecting me to be annihilated on the spot.

Dullin raised his arms heavenwards.

'Ah well. . . . If it's cholera,' he said, with a shrug – and turned to the business at hand: 'On stage, everyone back to work!'

Some people thought that Dullin, whose naïvety was

proverbial, had really been impressed by the heroism of an extra attending rehearsals even though racked by such a terrible disease. But I believe that he knew only too well that I was manipulating his ingenuousness. It provided him with an excuse for not taking disciplinary action against me. I had a special place in his heart. I made him laugh. He viewed me with the suspicion and curiosity of a cat which has found a mouse with six legs.

Dullin could switch from lyricism to innocence without a break. For his birthday the students gave him a wristwatch with phosphorescent numbers on the dial. The party was held on the stage. With some emotion he opened his little packet. 'Heavens above, a watch,' he said, as if he had just been given a Rolls-Royce.

'And do you know, sir, you can actually see the numbers in the dark?'

'Ah . . .' said Dullin. And with a grandiose gesture: 'Turn out the lights!'

Someone had to go to the central panel of switches and plunge the vast theatre into darkness, from the foundations to the gods. There was a respectful silence. Then, a full minute later, we heard Dullin announce in a disappointed little voice: 'I can't see anything. That's because it hasn't been wound up, I suppose.'

Propi, Gérald, my sister Hélène, Françoise and I were cycling along the roads of Normandy in search of ham, butter and eggs. Françoise was a girl I had just met at Dullin's classes. She was four years older than me. Between two unsuccessful forays to farms I confided to her that I was still a virgin. Out of a sense of pity she decided to put the finishing touches to my amorous education – the only area in which I was backward for my age.

A farmer put us up for the night in his barn. After a delicious meal of rabbit cooked on an oil stove we were all in euphoric mood. When the others had been asleep for hours, Françoise came to join me in my corner. Lying in the hay in the best tradition of popular songs, I graduated from adolescence to manhood. But just at the climax of my initiation something completely unexpected happened. The walls began to move. The ground trembled. The loose planks of the ceiling started to creak menacingly. An apocalyptic rumbling filled the air, the world seemed to be going mad. 'Christ,' I said to myself, 'I didn't know it could be like this!' Then when the planks in the ceiling started falling down on top of us I decided that it could only be the wrath of God. 'I've made a mess of it again,' I thought. But God had nothing to do with it all. I had unwittingly chosen to lose my cherry at one of the great moments of history: zero hour, 6 June 1944 – the first wave of the Allied landings in Normandy. We were only a few kilometres away from the coast. Every gun in the British and American navies' fleets had started up simultaneously and the German artillery was returning their fire.

7. First love

A friend introduced us. He was madly in love with her. She had green eyes, a Botticelli face and a golden white body. She was the most beautiful creature I have ever met. She was only sixteen, but already so naïvely indecent that, when aroused, she could take your breath away. She dressed like everyone else, but the only ornament she needed was her own naked body. The incarnation of sexuality. Perhaps inevitably this state of grace wasn't destined to withstand the ravages of time or man: ephemeral and fragile, a masterpiece of womanhood, she defied the laws of nature only for a brief moment. And I was lucky enough to be on the spot.

Her name was Nicole P——. The man who was dying of love for her had invited me to dinner with them so that he could savour his happiness all the better by showing her off.

But you don't take the Mona Lisa out for a walk on a lead. I stole her from him with my eyes and my voice. As soon as I sat down opposite her, I knew that fortune was going to smile on me. She looked at me – and she was already in my arms. If Jean-Claude took her hand clumsily, she touched her skin in a caress which was meant for me. If he told her that he loved her, her eyes repeated the same words for my benefit. Jean-Claude spoke of a journey and it was Nicole and I who were taking the boat or plane. He discoursed on the subject of sensuality while she silently promised me her thighs. I did not even touch her ankle under the table. Love at first sight is an undeniable fact: a perfect understanding which the disharmony of two personalities has not yet spoiled.

After dinner we took the Métro as far as the Porte

d'Italie and said goodbye to my friend at the entrance to his block of flats. It was the most cruel thing I have ever done in my life. And I did not feel the slightest remorse. We walked for a while and then took the Métro again to the chaussée d'Antin. She lived in the rue de Hauteville with her mother. I kissed her and went home. We had promised each other nothing. I slept calmly and happily. At about ten o'clock the next morning she rang me up and asked if she could come and live with me. I took a taxi to collect her and her luggage. She only had one small suitcase.

For some weeks I had been living in a furnished flat near the Porte de Saint-Cloud which I shared with my mother, my stepfather and my sister.

Who was it who said or wrote that lovers can only come to know each other and achieve perfect pleasure with the passage of time? There has to be an exception to every rule, and we set about proving it. The first night was the best, and so was the second, and the third and every one thereafter. I have known nothing to match it since. Making love is an activity in which I don't attach great importance to technique or experience. But I don't want to lay down the law, since in my opinion it's far better to let everyone get on with it in their own way – although that's not always as easy as it sounds. Most men and women today seem to get into bed together crammed with advice from Daddy, Mummy, the local policeman, the next-door neighbour, the Prime Minister, the moralist, the rabbi, or the vicar. Nicole and I were alone on our rumpled sheets and, if the proceedings were not conducted in strict accordance with social conventions or the tenets of Christianity, they were nevertheless not lacking in charm or interest.

At that time I was busy writing short stories of indeterminate style – a mixture of black humour and political satire. But I longed to undertake something on a grander scale. Psychology seemed to me a trivial and old-fashioned science which could be safely left to senile geniuses, and I had accordingly started to compose a novel which vacillated between the absurd and the pornographic.

Each morning Nicole would take my stepfather breakfast in bed. She would sit on the blankets and read him the latest pages of my novel: the story of Alfred Pastoureau, an inconsequential middle-class youth of no merit and little intelligence who would have ended his existence in irredeemable mediocrity had he not come to believe, as a result of two medical files getting mixed up, that he had a brain tumour. Convinced that he is going to die within six months, he becomes a depraved monster, betrays and kills his best friend, inherits his money by getting the lovely young widow accused of the murder, rapes her in prison, etc. .... As the story unfolds, inanimate objects – plants and furniture on which I bestowed the gift of speech – judge the abominable misdeeds of my hero according to their own standards – and, as a general rule, interfere in things which are none of their business.

I have never been much given to hypocrisy and the intimate scenes of the novel, although surrealistic, were described in meticulous detail. To be frank, some of the passages Nicole read out in her serious, childish voice would have made even an experienced adult's hair stand on end. But my stepfather had a great sense of humour and a sophisticated mind. He loved those morning readings. From time to time, Nicole would raise her eyes from the page to laugh heartily and wipe the coffee from Gérald's moustache: a charming family scene.

There were still ration books at that time and the only thing for which I reproached Nicole was that she never shared the biscuits or milk caramels which she sometimes brought back to the flat. During the day we hung around Saint-Germain des Prés, and we were often invited out to lunch or dinner. On Thursday and Sunday afternoons I earned a little money acting in a play for children. We lived a life of idleness and luxury. An Irish poet whose name I do not remember once described happiness as 'the thing which does not exist yet one day disappears'. I hate the way poets are always right.

Nicole had already had a lover. For a week she hardly referred to the matter. Her discretion made me uneasy, although I should have been delighted. But my instinct rarely deceives me. One day, without any obvious reason, she decided to talk about it.

'He is a monster,' she told me. 'I was madly in love with him.' (Suddenly chill, shiver, strange taste in the mouth.) 'He used to hit me and insult me. I used to stay indoors for days on end so that no one would see my bruises or my swollen lips. I cried so much that I had no more tears left. But I managed to get away from him. I can't remember how. When I met you, I had just finished convalescing. Emotionally, that is.'

'Are you cured?'

A pause.

'Are you cured?'

A pause.

'Yes.'

A 'yes' which I did not like.

She told me the man's name. A name without a face.

About ten days later she met him again. I was writing in the bedroom, annoyed that she was still out at two in the morning. When the bell rang I went to open the door and took her in my arms. Her kiss did not have the usual taste.

'I've seen him again,' she said.

'Yes.'

'I'm glad I've seen him again. Now I know that it's definitely all over. I'm cured. He was marvellous about it. I told him that I was in love with you. Instead of slapping me as I expected, he put his hands on my shoulders and told me that he was happy for me. You know, it's marvellous' ('marvellous' was one of her words) 'just to be friends with him.'

'Marvellous,' I said.

Two days later, to the hour, she was packing her few belongings in her orphan's suitcase. She did not seem happy to be going. Whenever I asked her a question or tried to get her to explain she replied:

'I don't understand . . .'

I did not want to be unkind to her. It was as if the life had been drained from her. Suddenly she had lost that joyful presence, that vitality which had made her such an exceptional creature.

'I don't understand,' she repeated.

She looked at me with empty eyes.

'Take my head in your hands. I don't want you to be angry. I wish he were dead, you know . . . but I can't get rid of him. He's waiting for me. Do you understand? . . . He's waiting for me.'

For the sake of understanding, I understood. What I have never understood, however, is the incredible importance women attach to being understood when they walk out on you. Personally, I always avoid the breaking-up scene in the most cowardly fashion. The end of a love affair is quite cruel enough without adding pointless formalities.

In the best tradition Nicole told me that she was the one who deserved the most pity. As she went through the door, she said:

'I'm going to cry in the taxi. I'm ashamed to tell you, but I think I'm going to cry.'

It seemed she had replenished her stock of tears.

I went with her as far as the taxi rank at the Porte de Saint-Cloud. She got into an ancient red G7 which took ages to start. The driver had a Russian accent and white beard, and looked like an ex-general of the White Army.

As a result of this episode in my life, I have remained eternally suspicious of the word 'friend' on a woman's lips. But at the time I had not yet learned to appreciate its full significance. I was profoundly unhappy.

My despair lasted for three days. And then suddenly, walking down the Champs-Élysées one sunny afternoon, I reacted violently against my feeling of powerlessness. Against the pain killing every other sensation. Against the deadness in my heart and head. 'Never, never again,' I promised myself. And I got over it just like that. To this day I still do not know by what effort of the will, by what intellectual stratagem, I managed literally to anaesthetize my love for Nicole. As a matter of fact, I don't really believe this was the best solution. What you think you have buried lives on in you, feeding on you silently. Gnawing away. It is just that you do not realize it.

I saw Nicole again eight years afterwards. She had changed; her soul, her body and even her name were different. She was a podgy, rather vulgar wreck who looked a good ten years older than she was.

She told me that she had wanted to come running back to me at least a hundred times, but had not dared to. That the taxi she had taken from the Porte de Saint-Cloud had been her coffin, its meter clocking up the price of her ignorance.

I asked her whether the driver had been Russian. She said she couldn't remember.

My apprenticeship in manhood had so far taken place under the Occupation. Now to complete the process, I found myself in the extraordinary world of Saint-Germain des Prés.

Much has been said about Saint-Germain des Prés and everything it stood for during the post-war years. No doubt one day the historians will give their own account of it. Of the men and women who actually lived through that period some are dead, some have rejected it, and others have been marked by it for life. One day perhaps someone will make a film about those mad events. It is not easy today to imagine how anyone could possibly survive in the middle of a large city without any money. Yet we lived like millionaires. It was a daily miracle.

People who had money spent it freely, those who had none were accepted without suspicion. There were no prejudices as regards class or sex, and not even any intellectual snobbery. A shared lifestyle united everyone.

It was about this time that I wrote a novel set partly in Saint-Germain des Prés. Looking for an opinion, I gave it to André Gide, who had a rather amused sort of affection for me. He claimed that I reminded him of Lafcadio, the hero of his novel *The Vatican Cellars*. He returned my manuscript with handwritten annotations. At the foot of the first page he had written 'Good'. On the third page 'Quite magnificent'. Thereafter the comments became rather less flattering.

My novel may not have been written in deathless prose, but it did give a reasonably faithful account of the atmosphere of Saint-Germain des Prés at that time – an atmosphere that didn't derive solely from Sartre, Boris Vian, the Rose Rouge or Adamov, but from a horde of adolescents of widely varying social and geographical origins. In the cafés and streets they lived out their anxieties or indifference together. It wasn't a place where one came to seek 'success' or to further one's education. On the contrary, it was a vast playground where people tried to allay their inevitable re-entry into society, their acceptance of the rule of respectable adult-life. Like the thought of death, the future was indefinitely postponed. (Misguided observers stuck the label of existentialism on us, but in fact Sartre's philosophical system didn't concern us in the slightest.)

Naturally, the problems of food, clothing and accommodation still had to be solved, but they did not condition our whole lives. We rejected all occupations which would have deprived us of our liberty, including those of parasite or sponger, but we found it natural to earn a little money whenever the opportunity arose. At one stage my sister was working as an extra on *Pétrus*, a film directed by Marc Allégret; she suggested that I might try my luck with him.

I got up early, put on the reversible lumber jacket which an American officer had given me and clocked in at the Francœur studios. The pay was two thousand francs a day. (That initial meeting with Marc Allégret was to determine my whole career, though of course I didn't realize it at the time.) The first evening my sister collected my pay as well as her own. The next day and for the following week we followed the same routine, but with one small difference: I decided that it was no longer necessary for me to turn up at the studios since my money was handed over so obligingly to Hélène. It seemed to me reasonable that cunning should be rewarded as much as work.

However, with his unfailing shrewdness, Allégret had spotted me among three hundred extras and soon found me out. Not that he made an issue of the matter – he simply wanted to carry on with a conversation which we had started on the set. He was an intelligent man, sensitive and cultivated, curious to learn about other people. He recognized merit in a human being, whether a stripper, a poet, a minister or a genius of the future. Being fascinated by youth, he scented talent before it had even had time to blossom. His finest epitaph will be the list of the names of those he helped at the beginning of their careers and who have become famous in one sphere or another.

Marc wanted to make a film about the post-war generation. He was surprised and delighted by what I had to tell him about my life and the young people I knew, and suggested that I write a screenplay based on my own experiences. This project would have remained no more than a vague dream if I hadn't discovered at the time that I was entertaining a parasite called *taenia solium* – otherwise known as the tapeworm. In the barbarous days of the early fifties getting rid of such unwanted tenants was a revolting business. You had to stay in bed for several days and submit to purgatives which would have knocked the stuffing out of a dray horse. Having nothing else to do

The Devil's work. Vadim directing *Les Bijoutiers du Clair de Lune* in Spain.

BARDOT. 'Endowed with an innate instinct for love.'

Opposite top: An early picture of Vadim with his future parents-in-law. Between Brigitte and Mme Bardot is her sister Mijanou. *Opposite right:* 20 December 1952. After three years Brigitte's parents allow her to marry Vadim at the age of eighteen. *Opposite far right:* Brigitte with a portrait of Vadim painted by herself.

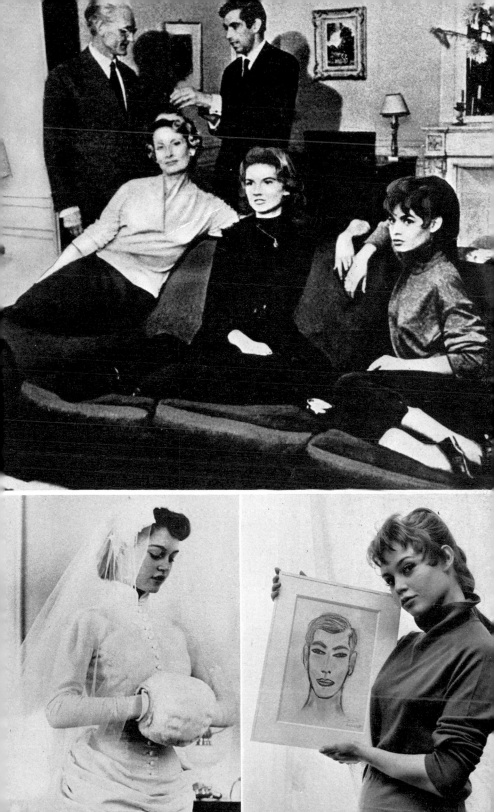

Above: . . . And Woman was Created, the film that made Vadim's reputation as a director and launched Brigitte as an international star. 'La sex-kitten' had arrived.

Left: Brigitte with Jean-Louis Trintignant with whom she fell in love during the shooting of the film.

From 1956 to 1976 the
Bardot look has retained
its appeal and influence
in Europe and America.

Left: Since the break-up of their marriage, Vadim and Bardot have remained close friends and have made several films together including, in 1974, *Don Juan* with Jane Birkin (*above*).

Right:
STROYBERG.
'Gentle, sensual and capricious.'

Above: Annette in her first film role playing the part of Mme de Tourvel in Vadim's controversial film of Laclos' erotic novel, *Les Liaisons Dangereuses.*

Left: Stardom gave Annette a taste for freedom. In 1959 she returned to Vadim after a brief romance with a pop singer. The reconciliation was not to last for long.

with myself, I wrote my first screenplay straight off, giving it the title *Les lauriers sont coupés*.

Marc liked the story and immediately found a producer for it, Pierre Braunberger. I had become the youngest screenplay writer in France. And perhaps in the world. A purely honorary title, however. The money which I received for an entire screenplay was equivalent to an unskilled worker's wages for three weeks. But it didn't matter. In those days money and a successful career were not the indispensable social criteria they are today. The table set by Gérard and Hervé Mille was equally lavish regardless of whether one was a prime minister, the Aly Khan, Marie-Hélène de Rothschild or the 'Steppenwolf' as they called me. Their mansion in the rue de Varenne, a focal point for the whole of Parisian society, was like a second home to me. Charm, youth and wit enjoyed the same privileges there as did fame and wealth. Another favourite haunt was the home of Pierre and Hélène Lazareff in Bourg-la-Reine, an exclusive meeting place for politicians, artists and journalists where I often spent my Sundays. Colette, whom I used to visit, also took a liking to me. Jean Cocteau wrote to me. I used to hang round the streets of Paris with Jean Genet who still had a life sentence hanging over his head at the time. I had a girl friend who was Ernest Hemingway's mistress. She used to insult him in restaurants in my presence – a habit which Hemingway seemed to find vastly amusing, roaring with laughter and tugging away at his beard.

I also met unknowns who were to become household names a few years later. I had no idea that the young American senator with whom I went swimming and had a lot of fun at the Hôtel du Cap, in Antibes, was going to become President John F. Kennedy.

One summer afternoon I was whiling away the time of day on the terrace of the Coupole with Christian Marquand. He noticed a strikingly handsome young man sitting near us. He had taken off his shoes and put his bare feet on the

C

table. He was stroking his toes voluptuously, saying over
and over again in English: 'That's great, that's just
great . . .' A conversation started. The young man told us
that he acted in the theatre in the United States and was
in Paris for a holiday. His name, Marlon Brando, was
unknown to us. That same evening he checked out of his
hotel to come and live with us in our little studio in the
rue de Bassano. He has been a close friend ever since.

Marlon had not yet made any films, but his performance
in Tennessee Williams's play *A Streetcar Named Desire* had
revolutionized Broadway. A week or two after our first
meeting the three of us were walking down the Champs-
Élysées at about five o'clock in the morning when
Marlon started to give a rendering of his part in *A Streetcar
Named Desire*. Warming to his task, he went through all
the parts in the play one by one. For an hour and a half,
without any scenery, props or costumes, he re-created the
magic of the theatre entirely on his own. We were dazzled,
fascinated. We did not even notice the day breaking. It
was then, before I had ever seen him on the screen, that I
discovered that Marlon Brando was not just a great actor
but a genius.

I doubt whether a boy of less than twenty arriving in
Paris today without any connections apart from a grand-
father working as a commission agent at Les Halles would
have any chance of living the kind of adventurous existence that I enjoyed after the Occupation. Nowadays
everyone expects men or women to be able to supply
tangible proof of their qualities. In other words, they must
be able to point to money or success. People have become
realists.

One might have expected that increasingly rapid means
of communication would have made the world a more
open place to live in, but this is just an illusion. The truth
is that our society is more divided than ever before. Para-
doxically, the age of the satellite and television has killed
social intercourse. We live in the era of slogans and

sectarianism, a return to tribalism, the sheep's instinct for security. Perhaps this was a necessary development. Sometimes, however, despite my natural optimism, I wonder where it will lead. I do not regret the past, but do not feel ready to live in a civilization constructed for and by a race of insects.

In 1949, however, I had other problems to worry about. I realized that my screenplay of *Les lauriers sont coupés* would never be filmed, despite Marc Allégret's reputation and the hectic dynamism of the producer, Pierre Braunberger. Nevertheless, something at least came out of that project.

Leslie Caron and Brigitte Bardot owe their careers to the tests they made for the film.

I had met Leslie Caron one day on the cross-Channel ferry and advised Marc Allégret to go and see Roland Petit's ballet *La rencontre*, in which she was currently appearing. On the screen, as on the stage, she had both charm and presence, but her inexperience worried the producer and she wasn't signed. Shortly afterwards, thanks to this test, she went off to Hollywood where a fabulous contract was awaiting her.

Contrary to popular belief, it wasn't I who discovered Brigitte Bardot. It was Marc Allégret, who noticed an item in *Elle* magazine in which Brigitte featured as the incarnation of the typical French girl. On Marc's suggestion I wrote to M. and Mme Bardot, 1 rue de la Pompe, Paris 16ème in the following terms: '. . . M. Marc Allégret would be delighted to meet your daughter Brigitte in connection with a project which he would like to discuss with you.' Mme Bardot was young and attractive. As an Aquarian, she must have had a liking for the unexpected and, despite her bourgeois prejudices and her husband's advice, she accepted the invitation.

'Elegance,' said Balzac, 'is appearing to be what one is.' This is not always easy for a young girl on the threshold of her fifteenth birthday. But Brigitte was born of the race of kings. She walked with the supple upright grace of a dancer, moved her head like a cat and her eyes followed every movement around her. She laughed easily, without timidity or aggressiveness. When her mother began to play the grand lady in the approved manner she interrupted with: 'Mummy, you're boring them stiff!' She was rather dark, wore no make-up and was simply dressed. While Mme Bardot imbibed the Allégret charm, Brigitte looked at me. She was puzzled but vaguely attracted by this thin taciturn boy who wore no tie, this character out of a Dostoievsky novel who nevertheless appeared to enjoy life. She walked out on to the balcony and surveyed the seventh-floor view of Paris. The sun was shining. I joined her.

'I love balconies,' she said.

'Why?'

'Do you have to have a reason for loving?'

Mme Bardot explained that her daughter wasn't really suited to the cinema but that she ought to have the chance of finding out for herself. She was a very good mother – a little old-fashioned, though she considered herself modern. She took the view that her daughter should go through her crisis of independence and then marry a diplomat or an engineer. It was decided that I would rehearse Brigitte once a week, on Wednesdays, after her dancing classes.

She arrived on time in the avenue Wagram. (At the time I was living with Daniel Gélin and his wife Danièle Delorme.) Brigitte was too independent to submit to the disciplines of diction and drama technique. But she could imagine a character in any situation, as long as that character was herself. I also used to go to see her at her dancing classes at the Walker school. There she was totally different. Wilting in her woollen leggings, she was a fragile but courageous figure, a creature made to fly. In their mirror work dancers watch themselves and correct their errors: with Brigitte one had the impression that the reflection was trying to imitate her. What a pity that she didn't display in the cinema the passion, fervour and discipline with which she approached dancing. By now, she would be one of the greatest actresses of all time. She often enjoyed acting, but never took it seriously. Dancing was her life, the cinema a game which she played well.

The day of the screen test arrived. I played opposite Brigitte and Marc reduced us to two dimensions with his camera's eye.

At the end of the day I took Brigitte home by taxi. A goodbye already. I didn't yet know that I loved her. She had been totally absorbed in me for some time, but had said nothing.

Braunberger was not overjoyed with the screen test and the shooting date was postponed once again. I was convinced that the film would never be made and was beginning to forget all about it. There were other things in life, and I was alive. Brigitte's face was gradually becoming no more than a vague memory.

And then one day, a Saturday, there came a turn in events. I am never bored, but that day I could think of nothing to do and nothing interested me. My flat-mates had gone away for the weekend and I was feeling oppressed by the empty flat in the avenue Wagram. The telephone had been cut off, Daniel Gélin having as usual paid no attention to the repeated reminders from the post office. I was out of money. I found some change in the kitchen and went down to the café in the place des Ternes to call for help. No one answered. Paris had abandoned me. I had one twenty-franc coin left! The price of a single telephone call. I do not know why I thought of Brigitte. She was elsewhere, in a Louis XVI flat in the *seizième arrondissement*, or more probably in Bougival in a Norwegian chalet imported from Oslo by some folksy aunt. And if by any chance I did get her on the telephone she would no doubt tell me that her parents were expecting friends to dinner and ask me to call again the following week. Despite all this, I sacrificed my last coin and dialled the number.

Brigitte answered and I announced myself. She asked me to come round, telling me that her parents had gone to Bougival, and that she was at the rue de la Pompe address with her grandmother and a friend, and was looking forward to seeing me. All of which meant: 'I am so glad you called. I'd given up hope. Come round. I haven't forgotten you. I can't stop thinking about you. When will you be here?'

The friend was a nice young man who had been Brigitte's boy friend the previous summer. He had lost all hope and was accepting the situation manfully. The grandmother was maintaining a discreet presence, allowing the children to play in the drawing-room. A delightful afternoon full of promise.

When I left, Brigitte came out on to the landing with me. In front of the open doors of the lift she put her lips to mine and we kissed.

She told me later that her grandmother had been worried about my clothes and long hair and had asked the friend to keep an eye on me when I left. She was afraid that I might take the silver away in my pockets.

8. Brigitte

Mirrors give an inverted image. When you look into one you don't notice this, but if you hold a page from a book up to the glass it becomes illegible.

With newspapers it is quite the opposite. You read back to front without realizing it. Very often it is the image suggested by the words which needs to be decoded.

The journalistic image of Brigitte and me, which enjoyed wide credence among the public, was one of debauchery, cynicism, social climbing and disdain for all moral rules. I was supposedly selling my love to the newspapers for a photograph on the third page, delivering up my wife to film producers so that I could watch from behind a two-way mirror, enjoy the show and collect the fabulous proceeds from the orgies on the set. She was a wanton woman who had sacrificed her body to the god of success, perpetuating the myth of the film world in which depravity pays better than talent.

Neither the newspapers nor their readers experienced the slightest qualms about what the truth might be. Why worry? It was more fun that way and, after all, people had to talk about something. A little spice goes a long way in conversations at such levels, and, as in Chinese cuisine, if it happens to be a little stale, so much the better.

Brigitte made *La Vérité* with Henri Georges Clouzot and *Vie Privée* with Louis Malle, two very good films which portrayed a young girl struggling almost obsessively with her quest for happiness, unable to cope with the contradictory demands of her natural sensuality and her overvulnerable heart. While she was modern in her shameless desire for freedom, her romanticism owed more to Madame Bovary. Louis Malle came close to the truth, but Clouzot achieved greater insight into her private life. But Brigitte managed to conceal one essential characteristic: her childishness. She had an obsessive need for people to be around her, to love her and to attend to her every whim. She had a child's difficulty in choosing between people and things that pleased her; she wanted everything all at once. She also possessed a capacity for switching instantly from the deepest despair to the most carefree happiness, but she was also deeply distrustful of the future, a concept she still finds difficult to grasp. She had a natural gift for lying, not in a malicious way, but in a simple and logical way which was designed to make life correspond to her wishes.

It is difficult for a child to conceive of a universe of which he is not the centre. Brigitte has created an artificial world which obeys her laws and gravitates around her. She is now over forty and has not stepped outside that world. Given this, her fear of children and lack of maternal instinct is not difficult to understand.

At fifteen she was a young girl who seemed to be ahead of her time. In rebellion against her parents' morality and milieu, endowed with an innate instinct for love, an aware and lucid mind and a fine sense of humour, she was very much an infant prodigy. But Mozart never grew up. This refusal to abandon the world of childhood is not the result of any intellectual limitations but of an education which was without doubt incompatible with her nature and emotional make-up. During her adolescence I could have helped her, but I didn't realize it. When I finally understood it was far too late.

When she stole a clandestine hour sandwiched between maths and dancing, psychology was not uppermost in my mind. It was more than I dared to accompany her to her doorstep. Her father used to wait on the seventh-floor balcony, watching the crossroads of the rue de la Pompe and the rue Paul Doumer to make sure that she came home without a boy friend. If she arrived after the regulation time he used to aim a handful of change at her from the balcony. She managed to get out of the way, but some passers-by were less fortunate.

Despite all this I got on very well with her parents. I found her mother, Toti, charming and intelligent. Pilou, her father, amused me with his irrational behaviour. He embodied, almost to the point of caricature, the virtues and intolerance of an outmoded middle class. He was a likable fellow bedevilled by a bad temper. He always wanted to do the right thing and always got it wrong. To the exasperation of his family and the delight of everyone else, he had a gift for saying the wrong thing at the wrong time. He used to write down funny stories in a little book which he liked to produce at meals. He would always get the punch lines wrong without realizing it and then burst into tears of laughter.

I believe that Pilou and Toti were very fond of me. They found me well behaved, but their main complaint was that I did not earn a steady living. To be a bohemian was one thing, but to be poor into the bargain was beyond the pale. I was allowed to meet Brigitte at the flat and take her to the cinema with a chaperon. This role was sometimes played by Mijanou, her younger sister, who used to sneak on us when we arrived home: 'Vadim kissed Brigitte in the Métro.' On such occasions Brigitte was forbidden to see me for a week.

We met secretly for a year. Her parents sometimes went away for a weekend. For Brigitte a night was worth a lifetime. But this constant tension was too much for her. She could think only of her love. The walls of her bedroom had become a prison. She used to cry for hours on end. One morning I went to her dancing school while she was having a lesson. She wasn't expecting me. She was standing on tiptoe, doing pirouettes and crying all the while. Boris Kniazeff, her dancing master, beat on the floor with his baton and exclaimed: 'But you're crying! For goodness' sake, you're crying!' He was very angry.

'My feet hurt,' said Brigitte. And she went on crying.

'A dancer always has sore feet! But she forgets about it. Dancing is a joy. A joy!' He tapped out: 'One, two, three, *jeté*! One, two, *attitude*! . . . Smile! . . . One, two, *saut de chat*! . . . Smile!'

Brigitte tried to smile, danced, and cried even more. 'I wish you had to put up with it!'

'Put up with what?' roared Kniazeff.

'What I have to put up with at home, my father on my back all the time.'

'That isn't dancing! When you dance, you forget everything. I order you to forget all that! One, two . . . *attitude*! . . . *jeté battu*! . . .' But the tears continued to flow. 'My goodness, it's the Don! It's the Dnieper! It's the Volga! You haven't come here for the drama classes. This is a dancing school!'

Twenty minutes later she was in my arms. The tears had disappeared, but her eyes implored: 'Vadim, I can't stand it any longer. I can't go on. Please, do something. Poor Sophie is suffering too much. She can't go on living like this. . . .'

Sophie was the name of the heroine of a novel which I had written several months before my first meeting with Brigitte. Nevertheless, Brigitte had much in common with her, particularly in her turns of phrase. Brigitte used to sign her love letters 'Sophie' and often identified herself with the character.

I could only implore her to be patient. Her father would have had me thrown into prison rather than let us live together. He was, of course, blissfully unaware that I was seeing her secretly. Toti did not believe that her daughter was my mistress, but she was beginning to suspect something.

About the time Brigitte reached her sixteenth birthday I moved into 16 Quai d'Orléans. A small furnished room with a narrow bed, a chair, a deal table and a window overlooking the roofs of the Île Saint-Louis. It was about as romantic as you could get, but a little short on comfort. My close friend Christian Marquand lived in the room next door. At the end of the attic passage were the quarters of Li Phang, our Chinese cook.

We had found Li Phang in tears in a Montparnasse café. He was drowning his sorrows in red wine, having been sacked on the previous day for drunkenness. We employed him on a trial basis, using more or less everything I had just been paid for a commentary for a film by Haroun Tazieff on volcanoes to pay his wages. We were delighted with this arrangement, apart from two minor details: we had no kitchen and Li Phang's name was Michel. It seemed unreasonable to sink virtually all my capital into the acquisition of a Chinese cook whose name was Michel, so we informed him that henceforth he was to be called Li Phang. At first he would have none of this, but when advised that it was a *sine qua non* of the job he reluctantly accepted it. Not entirely, however, for he cheated a little by announcing himself as 'Li Phang, formerly Michel'. The problem of the kitchen was more easily resolved. Pending better days, Li Phang had to brew the coffee in the morning on a spirit stove, make the beds and sweep the corridor. He swore never to drink again and never kept his word. He used to hide his bottles in our landlord's flat, usually in the lavatory cistern, much to the consternation of the plumber who was called in every three days or so. But, as Christian used to say, 'If you take on staff, you take on the problems with the advantages.'

One morning, at about ten, there was a knock on the door. An anguished voice announced: 'This is Li Phang, formerly Michel. Come quickly! Tragedy on the line.' I worked out that this meant that there was a call for me on the telephone in our landlord's flat. It was Brigitte in a state of total panic. 'It's dreadful! Daddy is going to kill you!' She was calling from home and could not say any more. She asked me to meet her at her dancing school and put the receiver down.

Brigitte arrived early. Apparently her father had come into her room that morning with a gun and said: 'You see this revolver. If I ever discover that you are Vadim's mistress I shall kill him with it.' She had been too taken aback to protest and Pilou had walked out without another word. By the time she had recovered, he had left for the office. She had rushed to her mother, who was putting on her make-up.

'Mummy, Daddy's gone mad.'

'Again?' replied Mme Bardot calmly.

'He said that if I was Vadim's mistress, he would kill him.'

'Are you his mistress?'

'Of course not, Mummy. Who do you take me for?'

'Then what are you afraid of?'

'I don't know . . . Someone might tell him stories – and you know him! You must do something, Mummy.'

'Well,' answered Toti, 'if ever you were stupid enough to do such a thing and your father didn't have the courage to kill Vadim, I would do the job myself.'

For the second time that morning Brigitte was at a loss for words.

'Your parents have no intention of killing me,' I told Brigitte. 'They simply want to frighten you out of becoming my mistress.'

'Mummy perhaps. But Daddy wasn't joking, I'm absolutely sure of it.'

She was so convinced that in the end I began to believe her.

There was nothing I could do to cheer her up and she was still worried about it weeks later.

I wonder to this day what would have happened if M. Bardot had found out the truth.

9. A sex kitten is born

We were living a pointless tragedy. Brigitte's parents thought that they were helping her by preventing her from doing something stupid. They had not realized that she was very much in love and that age has nothing to do with the intensity of such a passion. Parents have never been convinced by the story of Romeo and Juliet, despite the box-office returns.

For three years and two months Brigitte begged her parents to accept our love for each other. She was in tears almost every day. On one occasion she even tried to kill herself. But nothing could shake their resolution: she could marry me at eighteen, and not before. They were convinced that she would forget me or that I would tire of waiting. They were wrong. But it was too much for Brigitte to bear. Three years is a very long time when you are young. Something in Brigitte broke and she has never been the same since. I have kept more than a hundred of her letters, many of which are illegible in places, the words smudged with her tears. Even after twenty-five years I am still moved when I read them.

A few months after the revolver business I decided to take refuge at a villa my mother had rented in the hills outside Nice. I planned to get down to writing a screen-play – life in Paris might have been cheap, but I found it difficult to work seriously there.

On the evening of my departure I went to say goodbye to Brigitte at the rue de la Pompe. I found her very upset. For some trivial reason her parents had threatened never to let her see me again. I consoled her by telling her that they were not serious, and that they would have forgotten about it by the time I returned. She was unhappy but very calm, which was not typical of her in such circumstances. I should have realized that something was wrong, but instead I simply thought that she was learning to be more reasonable.

On the landing she looked at me for a long time without speaking. I have never forgotten her deeply unhappy expression. It seemed to be saying: 'I know, my darling. There is nothing you can do. And nothing I can do. I'm sorry. I have tried to be reasonable. I can't go on. I simply can't go on.' I got into the lift and the door closed between us.

By the time I reached the train, I was full of misgivings. I was haunted by the look in Brigitte's eyes. At La Roche Migène, where the train stopped for water, I almost got out. But I hadn't yet learned to recognize the instinctive feeling I was always to get whenever Brigitte was in serious danger, whatever the distance between us.

It was only several days later that I learnt what had happened, from a letter written by Brigitte.

Her parents had gone out with Mijanou towards nine in the evening to see the Paris monuments under their new lighting. Brigitte wrote a note to her parents, put the envelope on the kitchen table, turned on the gas, knelt down and put her head in the oven. M. and Mme Bardot came home two hours earlier than anticipated to pick up a coat for Mijanou, who had felt cold. Brigitte was already unconscious and had to be revived with oxygen. Her parents' initial reaction was the conventional one: 'How could you do a thing like this to us!' Pilou threatened to despatch her to boarding school in England. But Toti met the situation with more common sense and promised her daughter next day that she could marry me after her eighteenth birthday.

When I returned from Nice, Brigitte decided to give up the dancing career which was her fondest dream, but nevertheless came second to her love for me. She realized that a professional dancer cannot have any real family life. For her, signing her first film contract was a sacrifice. She was never really interested in filming and anyway one must admit that films like *Manina, fille sans voile* and *Le trou norman* weren't exactly inspiring. Nevertheless she was making a name for herself. She was beginning to attract the attention of newspapermen. People talked about Brigitte Bardot, if not about the parts she played. Later, an explanation was found for the enormous appeal she had for the press: it was put down to my Machiavellian genius for publicity. Nothing is further from the truth. I sometimes advised her, but I never whispered clever answers into her ear or got in touch with editors to suggest coverage. No, it was her own natural instinct. A mixture of rudeness and friendliness, plus a lot of earthy common sense. ('What was the best day in your life?' Answer: 'It was a night.') She was neither too remote nor too familiar in her attitude. A woman's promises from the face of a child. An adolescent with a body cast from the same mould as the Venus of Milo. And that unique presence which made people's heads turn when she entered a room, even before they had seen her.

She was completely unknown in England when she was booked to make *Doctor at Sea* in London with Dirk Bogarde. The producers organized a press conference in a room in the Dorchester Hotel on the day she arrived. Three reporters, hard up for copy, and a few under-employed photographers turned up – more for the whisky and sandwiches than out of a sense of professional duty. Her magnetism did its work. They discarded the buffet in favour of the little French girl whom they christened 'the sex kitten'. By the next day, all the English papers had front-page photographs of Brigitte, relegating the traditional lion cubs and stray dogs to oblivion. A miracle which no star could have worked.

At Cannes a visit to an American aircraft carrier and the admiring wolf whistles of two thousand marines brought the film festival to the attention of the world who

normally ignored it. For ten years starlets had been sub-
mitting to the ritual of visiting the battleships standing off
Cannes without arousing any more reaction than an item
in the festival bulletin or a page three photograph in
Nice-Matin.

In Rome she played a minor role as a maidservant to
Helen of Troy in an Italian-American super-production.
Rosanna Podesta was the star of the film, but it was
Brigitte who was chased by the *paparazzi* whenever she
walked out of a trattoria on the Via Veneto. The period
hadn't yet arrived when every office girl would transform
herself into a poor man's BB, nor was she the mistress of a
politician or a famous actor, but everyone was talking
about her. Nobody even knew that she had just married
a poor unknown journalist.

To be allowed to marry Brigitte I was obliged to comply
with two conditions imposed by her parents. First, I had
to become a Catholic and, second, I had to get a job with
a regular monthly salary. My religious instruction under
the tutelage of a local priest was more picturesque than
practical, but it represented no hardship. Because I
belonged to the Orthodox faith, the priest exempted me
from baptism on condition that I promised to bring up
our children as Catholics. However, when it came to
finding a job, I couldn't make up my mind. I had already
forsworn a career in the diplomatic service and a manual
job wouldn't have gone down too well with my parents-
in-law. I had no gift for commerce and lacked the necessary
training to be successful in industry or finance.

I decided to go and see my friend Hervé Mille, who was
then with *Paris-Match*. He took me on as a rewriter at
the monthly salary of 80000 old francs plus bonuses. But
I really wanted to be a reporter, chiefly because of the
element of the unexpected and for the expense account –
and I soon had my wish. Television had not yet usurped
magazines as far as news reporting was concerned and I
have wonderful memories of my three months of journal-

ism. I met tramps and kings, madmen and geniuses; I
survived war, death, disaster and official banquets – and I
formed some of the closest friendships of my life. We were
a real gang at *Paris Match*. We had our own moral code,
our own jokes, our own vocabulary. It wasn't easy to gain
access into our little circle. There were about fifteen of us,
of whom more than half are now dead. Jean Roy, the
maddest of all, killed at the wheel of his jeep on the Suez
Canal; Jean-Pierre Pedrazzini, the most handsome of men,
mortally wounded in Budapest; Eric Bromberger, so witty
and so gifted, killed when he fell down the stairs of the
magazine's offices at five in the morning; André Frédérique,
the poet, dead by his own hand. Of the others, one was
blown up by a mine in Indochina, another was killed in a
road accident and another died in an air crash.

To earn social acceptability I had agreed to get a job
and to my surprise found myself in the middle of an
adventure, a member of journalism's last commando. I
miss my friends, I still mourn them; with them a certain
style of life, a certain kind of courage and pride disappeared for ever.

On 20 December 1952 Brigitte became Mme
Plémiannikov at the town hall in the avenue Henri Martin
in Paris, in the presence of a lady mayor who made a long
speech on Franco-Russian friendship in a world united
in peace and tolerance. M. Bardot wanted to protest that
his daughter was not marrying a foreigner, but his wife
tugged pointedly at his sleeve and he reluctantly kept
quiet. Brigitte could hardly suppress her laughter. It was
a very successful ceremony.

We were due to travel down to the Alps the next day
and on our return were going to move into a little flat in
the rue Chardon-Lagache which M. and Mme Bardot had
lent us. So I spent my first night of married life at my
in-laws' flat in the rue de la Pompe. Brigitte was in bed in
her nightdress and I was holding her hand. At eleven
o'clock her father left us, saying: 'I'm leaving you together

for ten minutes. After that, Vadim, you go to the dining-room, where I have had the camp bed put up.'

At first Brigitte thought it was a joke. When she realized that her father was serious she almost choked with indignation: 'It's up to me to decide where my husband is going to sleep!' 'What husband?' came the reply. 'But . . . him, of course,' she replied unbelievingly, pointing to me. Very dignified, very calm, M. Bardot pointed out that a town hall marriage was no more than a pagan formality inherited from the Revolution, and that the real ceremony would take place the next day at ten o'clock, before God in the church at Auteuil. Until then, he declared, we were not married – and he went out of the room without waiting for any comment from his daughter. It was all I could do to dissuade Brigitte from decamping immediately to the nearest hotel. We had waited patiently for three years, why break with her family now over a few hours more? She resisted stubbornly: 'It's a matter of principle.' 'Leave principles to your father,' I told her, 'he's more at home with them than you.' She agreed in the end, we laughed it off and, when our ten minutes were up, I abandoned my young wife to solitary meditation on morality, religion and life in general.

The next day I said 'Yes' for the second time in the church. My mother had tears in her eyes. Marc Allégret, my best man, was deeply moved and, after God had given us His blessing, M. Bardot added his. It was a fairy-tale ending.

After a very cheerful reception we drove south. A few kilometres beyond Fontainebleau, Brigitte began to cry. I hoped it was happiness. But she shook her head.

'I'm frightened,' she said.

10. The Devil wore a halo

The struggle for the right to live together had exhausted us more than we realized; the patience and understanding needed in the early stages of a marriage had all been used up. It is the daily process of discovering the impulses of each other's body and mind that enable a couple to get over their first disagreements and learn to live in harmony. Passion must last long enough to allow love to grow. If it dies too quickly, before there can be a marriage of souls, complete mutual understanding and the comfort of familiarity, the two people find themselves alone, driven by obscure desires and lost dreams.

I see passion as a boat in which two people play and make love without noticing in their carefree happiness that there is a hole in the bottom. Their eyes are turned towards their destination, a beach holding out the promise of hot white sand and shady trees. Day after day, week after week, the boat draws nearer the shore where they will live happily ever after, safe from the uncertainties of sea and weather. But the boat usually sinks before they reach the shore.

For us, the boat trip had already lasted too long. The beach that Brigitte dreamed of was an impossible paradise. When the tide finally carried us ashore she didn't recognize it. She had expected to be happy every second of the day and couldn't understand why there were insects, wind and rain, or that the fruit on the trees wasn't ripe all year round. She saw life with me as a cake called 'happiness' which she could eat day and night, winter and summer, awake or asleep. She used to sulk in the morning when I had been unkind to her in her dreams. This obsession with happiness was to become crucial with Brigitte. It was inevitable that sooner or later she would hold me responsible for the fact that the world did not fit the image of her fantasies.

And yet the flat in the rue Chardon-Lagache lent to us by my parents-in-law was a delightful little love-nest. Sunshine, a romantic wrought-iron balcony, an adorable old concierge straight out of a de Maupassant novel and her nightingale, Tino, straight out of a cartoon. There were a few minor drawbacks, however: the dustbins had to be taken up and down three flights of stairs every day, the balcony overlooked a police station and Tino only sang once a year, and then in the raucous tones of a crow. To begin with we had no telephone, no tables, no chairs, no curtains, and we slept on a mattress on the floor. Brigitte would buy furniture in the flea market – an English desk, *directoire* armchairs – and, on my return, ask: 'Haven't you noticed anything?' I would look around and say: 'You've cut your fringe.' Although I am very fussy over scenery and props when making a film, I have never been able to take an interest in my own surroundings. I only notice furniture and pictures if I don't like them – a characteristic which, of course, Brigitte held against me.

She became the perfect housewife, indignant over the price of chops, irritated by dry-cleaning bills. Although she wasn't a miser, she could be obsessively penny-pinching about small things. For example, she would spend three days looking for a shop where the material for a bedspread was sixty francs cheaper. In the process she would manage to spend five thousand francs on taxi fares and then announce proudly: 'You're lucky to have a wife who's so careful over money.' But she was also extremely generous when it came to helping a friend who was ill or saving a dog (she was already passionately fond of animals but, unlike today, did not yet consider them more worthy of her attention than people). Her humani-

tarian instincts were very strong: I remember that when
the Rosenbergs were executed we were up all the previous
night writing political articles in exercise books. The next
day I took her to Orly to catch a plane to London where
she was due to finish a film; as we drove to the airport,
she threw hundreds of pieces of paper out of the car
window with slogans on them like 'Eisenhower assassin',
'Save the Rosenbergs' and 'Ike = Stalin'.

We quarrelled frequently, sometimes violently, and the
periods between the moments of deep tenderness and
rediscovered passion grew longer and longer. But, on the
whole, we were quite happy together. We had a lot of
friends and our parties in the rue Chardon-Lagache were
always lively. On the other hand, Brigitte was shy about
going out. She would decide that she wasn't pretty,
spending hours in front of her mirror fiddling with her
hair, changing her dress or blouse a dozen times and often
collapsing in tears, leaving me to make excuses at the last
minute. She found it difficult to understand her success on
the screen and the biggest compliment she would ever pay
herself was an occasional 'I'm quite pretty today'. Although she loved to wield her power of attraction over
men, she remained faithful for several years – as far as I
am aware. At the risk of disappointing some readers and
compromising my reputation I have to admit that we
were generally monogamous and had very little penchant
for the conjugal extravaganzas in fashion today.

Let me quote an example, an occasion when we found
ourselves in the Rome of the *dolce vita*. Ursula Andress
had run away from her boarding school in Switzerland to
be with Daniel Gélin, for whom she had lost her seventeen-
year-old head and her innocence. After a few hectic weeks
(one needed a stout constitution to keep up with the
frenzied pace of life with Daniel) the grand passion began
to wilt. Ursula came to seek refuge in our hotel room. We
only had one double bed and, as the weather was very
hot, Brigitte, Ursula and I slept in the nude. In the

morning we breakfasted out on the sunlit balcony overlooking the seven hills. Brigitte and Ursula leant laughing,
suntanned and naked, over the balcony to throw bread
crusts down on to the passers-by in the Via Sistina. It was
delightful to behold and I wonder how many saints would
have been safe from eternal damnation had they found
themselves in my position. And yet . . . I did not allow
myself one little kiss. During the week Ursula spent with
us the innocent gaiety of our *ménage à trois* was not
marred by the slightest dubious gesture. To be candid, it
was not for lack of inclination, but I knew that Brigitte
would not have appreciated fraternization of that nature,
so the Devil wore his halo to bed.

Brigitte and Ursula loved to be told fantastic stories. In
bed I would spin them tales about vampires, succubi and
incubi. They squealed and hid under the sheets. I thought
that it was merely fun, but when we got back to Paris,
Brigitte refused to stay in the flat alone after nightfall.
When I had to work late at *Paris-Match* she used to wait
for me, huddled in the car, sometimes until five in the
morning. I was afraid that she would catch cold and
bought her a cocker spaniel puppy, which she christened
Clown, to protect her from 'monsters'.

Without being a star, Brigitte was already well known
and I was often called 'M. Bardot'. I decided that it was
time for me to make a name for myself as well. I asked the
magazine for indefinite leave to devote all my time to the
cinema. A year later *Cette sacrée gamine* had been completed, with both the screenplay and the script by me. It
was Michel Boisrond's first film. We had booked Dary
Cowl, Jean Poiret, Michel Serrault and Françoise Fabian,
newcomers to the screen, to work with Brigitte. It was a
success and I wrote another comedy for Marc Allégret,
En éffeuillant la marguerite, again with Brigitte, who
seemed to be specializing in comedy characters. I was
enormously successful as a writer, but it didn't occur to
producers to invite me to direct. I was twenty-six years old

and, at the time, youth was not a marketable commodity.

The next important step in my career came as a result of my affiliation with the producer Raoul Lévy. The first time we met each of us felt a strong affinity for the other, and we decided right away to make a film together. There are always the men who, out of imagination, chance or necessity, find themselves in the right place at the right time. There are the people who provoke the accidents which change everything. By rejecting fashion, they create fashion. Raoul Lévy was such a person. He was incapable of resting, a man who tossed a thousand ideas around in his head, followed up ten of them, rejected all of them and then stuck to the thousand and first until he turned it into a success. Masochistic and tyrannical, attractive and repulsive, he had a genius for making people forgive him for everything and the gift of the great Renaissance Florentines for loving and betraying at the same time. I cursed him a thousand times and loved him faithfully until that grotesque morning when he pointed a double-barrelled shotgun at himself and pulled the trigger. That day those of us who loved him lost a brother and French cinema was orphaned.

In 1955 Raoul was a hard-up young producer and I was a novice writer. Our first project together brought shrugs of disbelief from film people, who advised us to buy a lottery ticket instead. Even before we had decided what the film was going to be about we announced that Brigitte Bardot would play the lead, which didn't help matters. The stars of the day were Michèle Morgan, Martine Carole, Dany Robin and Françoise Arnoul. Nevertheless, Raoul found a producer who had confidence in my potential as a director. Famous before the war for his college boys' band, Ray Ventura was brilliantly successful in the cinema. And in agreeing to co-produce our film (which did not yet even have a title) he displayed flair and courage. As far as the screenplay was concerned I knew what I wanted to say, but I needed a plot. One day Raoul

Lévy mentioned a recent news item: three brothers, a village, a beautiful woman, a crime – and . . . *Et Dieu créa la femme* was born.

At that time, as I have said, the idea of allowing a young man to direct was absurd. To decide to film an intimate drama in cinemascope and colour was pure quixotic fantasy. By tradition, it had to be black and white, and the ordinary-size screen. Wide-screen projection – although a French invention – was strictly for multi-million-dollar Hollywood productions and Technicolor was for Esther Williams and swimming pools or musical comedy. The French were still sceptical about their use. At the Cannes Festival that year the jury awarded the Grand Prix to the black and white *Marty*, well acted and well made perhaps, but more suitable for television – while the magnificent *East of Eden*, made by Elia Kazan in colour and cinemascope with James Dean in his best role, did not even receive a consolation prize. But I had my own ideas about close-ups on the wide screen and the use of colour to achieve dramatic effect.

Raoul Lévy understood what I was trying to do and decided to back me all the way. Ray Ventura didn't have all the money, but nothing could stop Raoul once he had the bit between his teeth. One morning at eight o'clock the telephone rang in the rue Chardon-Lagache.

'Are you awake?' Raoul asked.

'No.'

'Can you pack a bag in your sleep?'

'Never tried. Might as well find out.'

'Good. I'll be waiting for you at the Gare de l'Est at ten-forty. We're taking the Munich express.'

'Why the express? And why Munich?'

'I'll explain,' said Raoul.

I packed my bag in my sleep and dressed in record time for a zombie.

In the train Raoul told me what he was up to.

'We're going to book Kurt Jurgens.'

Kurt Jurgens was already an internationally famous star by then.

'For what film?'

'Ours.'

'I see,' I said. 'Which part?'

'Christian Marquand's.'

'Are they both going to play the same part?'

'Does it bother you?' answered Raoul.

'It's not the fact that there are two of them that bothers me, it's the question of age. The elder brother is twenty-five. Kurt Jurgens is forty. Five years less than his mother in the film.'

'Yes, it's rather awkward,' acknowledged Raoul.

'And what about a Saint-Tropez fisherman speaking with a German accent? That's going to be a bit odd, isn't it?'

'Well, yes.'

'Are you sure we need him?'

'Columbia will give us the money to make the film in Cinemascope and colour if we can get Jurgens.'

'That still strikes me as being difficult.'

'You're right,' Raoul agreed. 'It was a bad idea.'

We decided to have lunch in the restaurant car and get off the train at the next stop. But since it was an express there were no more stops before the border. And that gave Raoul time to think of another solution.

'And what if we wrote in a part for him?'

'It could only be a walk-on part. Do you really believe that a big star is going to accept a small part in a film by an unknown director with a starlet in the leading role?'

'I don't know. But we can try. There's no such word as impossible in the French language.'

'You're Belgian and I'm half Russian,' I pointed out.

'No one knows I'm Belgian and you were born in Paris.'

'True.'

We did not get off at the border, but went straight to the best hotel in Munich.

Raoul did not know Jurgens, but before even opening his suitcase he had talked him into a meeting for the day after next.

'You've got forty-eight hours to rewrite the screenplay,' he told me. 'Sixty pages will be enough.'

'Thank you,' I replied, 'you're too kind.'

To prevent me from succumbing to the urge to go out in search of temptation, Raoul brought the temptations into the room. Caviar, smoked salmon, vodka. And Maria. Maria was dark, tall and well rounded in hips and bosom. Raoul refused to tell me her price, reminding me that a gentleman does not discuss how much his presents cost. Before I could even pull the top off my biro, Maria had undressed. I must have looked worried, because she asked me if she should put her stockings or her suspender belt back on. I told her that that wasn't the problem, but that I had forty-eight hours in which to do three weeks' work. She spoke French quite well and I told her about my screenplay. She loved the idea and suggested that I make the heroine a more sympathetic character by showing her to be unselfish despite her loose morals. 'If she's not interested in money,' said Maria, 'people won't think she's a tart.'

Developing this idea, I visualized a rich, attractive man fascinated by my heroine. Money had helped him to seduce the most inaccessible women, but this little waif who was so generous with her body wasn't the least bit interested in his bank account. While Maria waved her suspender belt about in the excitement of creation, the part for Jurgens began to take shape in my mind.

Maria had done a secretarial course, but a typist's pay had given her little opportunity to indulge her passion for cars, and she had acquired bad habits as she progressed from a Volkswagen to a Mercedes. Her ultimate objective was a Lincoln Continental, and she swore that when she had one she would go back on to the straight and narrow.

'When you have a Lincoln,' I told her, 'you will want a chauffeur-driven Rolls.'

'Oh no! I wouldn't have a chauffeur,' she retorted indignantly. 'I like driving too much.'

She offered to type my text as I wrote it. I accepted gratefully. She asked if I minded if she put her clothes back on to perform her new duties. I agreed. I never saw Maria's suspender belt again, but the sixty pages of the new screenplay had been typed in triplicate and corrected by the following evening. I thanked her and apologized for having contributed so little towards her Lincoln Continental.

'I'm in no hurry,' she said. 'And anyway, it is I who should be thanking you. I've never enjoyed myself so much.'

As Raoul commented, that was class.

Kurt Jurgens, who was finishing off a film, met us at the studio. After filming he took us to his house in the country. I gave him the story-line without making his part sound more important than it was and gave him the sixty-page text. Raoul pointed out that we could not wait for his answer until the screenplay was finalized. This was not the usual way of doing things, but Jurgens' interest was aroused. He was a sensitive man and more intelligent than his rather brash manner would lead one to suppose. And there would obviously be no question about his taste and judgement, since he trusted me on sight and gave his agreement in writing that same evening. He liked the south of France, and the idea of filming with Brigitte Bardot and trying out a new type of film appealed to him. He wasn't bothered about playing a minor part.

I still feel a great deal of friendship and gratitude towards Kurt Jurgens. No other big star has ever shown such confidence in me. I have contributed to the success of many actors and actresses, and actually even created the careers of some of them, but once they had become famous, none of them have ever risked agreeing to film with me without having first seen and approved a com-

D

pleted screenplay. And even then the answer often depended on how successful my previous films had been.

If miracles only happen once, this one could not have happened at a more opportune moment. By the time we got back to the hotel with Curt Jurgens's contract in our hands, even Raoul, who usually expected the impossible to happen, couldn't believe that we'd succeeded.

11. I'm not superstitious, it's unlucky

The first time she met Jean-Louis Trintignant, Brigitte pulled a face. 'How do you expect me to play a love scene with him?' she screamed at Raoul and me. 'He's too small. He's ugly. And in any case he's not my type.'

Five weeks after we started filming . . . *Et Dieu créa la femme* she was in love with him. It had happened. The deep passion of the young girl who wanted to die for me, the promises of 'always', the nights, the body I loved, the secrets, the times when we wanted to be left alone – all that was over.

I had not expected it to be Jean-Louis Trintignant, but I had been preparing myself for this moment for over a year. Now I wanted our first film to take the place of the child we had not had. I wanted it to be the seed and the fruit of seven years of tumult and hope. The parting of the ways, rather than the end of the road. Until we started filming, Brigitte got more and more depressed every day. She was in mourning for her happiness. But, despite everything, I was at peace with myself when shooting began. I had reconciled myself to the inevitable and in a way I was looking forward to regaining my freedom. I knew Brigitte well enough to realize what she was feeling in her partner's arms before she did. On the set it didn't affect me. I have never been affected by personal feelings when directing a scene. Even if I know the actors intimately, they remain an abstraction for me while I am working. They are to me what figures are to a mathematician, nothing more. I am completely immune to nudity or the most erotic scenes. In my private life I am prey to violent and conflicting emotions if I see the woman I love in the arms of another man – but in bed on a film set, never. People can understand that Alfred Hitchcock doesn't share the criminal's enjoyment when he directs a murder scene, so why can't they see that I manage to remain similarly detached when I watch Jane Fonda rolling about on a bathroom floor with Peter McEnery?

This confusion between fiction and reality, between working life and private life, probably explains the popular image of me as a cynical, perverted voyeur. I feel like adopting André Gide's comment on the journalists who misrepresented him: 'They have given me a hump on my back and now they are wearing themselves out pummelling it.' In *La Curée*, for instance, Jane Fonda's naked breasts can be seen for twenty-five seconds. In another scene, lasting one minute, her distorted, fluid, abstract reflection can be seen in the vinyl on the bathroom wall while she is supposed to be making love. On reading the press reviews (which were not all unfavourable) I learned that I showed my ex-wife nude and in every imaginable position throughout the whole film. One wonders what the critics were doing for the other 103 minutes!

We live in an unsubtle age. The tidal wave of information which floods over the public has to be categorized immediately, and once the label has been stuck on, there's no time left for the finer details. It was the shooting of my first film in Nice and Saint-Tropez that set the wheels of the myth machine in motion and they have been turning steadily ever since. Portraying my wife in love with another man, playing with her emotions and, above all, showing her naked in the arms of her lover – I was really doing the newspapermen's job for them. I hoped that they would see a Pirandello situation in it all, but I was forgetting how editors' minds work. Magazines live off scandal at the expense of its victims and for a certain element of the press the truth is only of interest in so far as it serves as a prop for an exaggerated, distorted story. So, instead of Pirandello, we had Rasputin. Out of

Machiavellianism, I had, apparently, thrown Brigitte into her partner's arms. I wasn't making a film, but the sauce to go with the inevitable scandal. I was a sado-masochistic voyeur wallowing in the prospect of the subsequent tumult which would also help to swell the profits. The idea that I could be a victim of circumstance and hadn't deliberately provoked this situation was less commercial from the journalistic point of view and therefore disregarded.

In fact, I was rather sad. Brigitte was living with me in the Hôtel Négresco. We had agreed that we would continue to live together until the film had been completed. But Trintignant decided to play the tyrannical lover. He wanted a proof of her love, a sacrifice, and threatened that he would never see Brigitte again if she didn't leave me immediately. His attitude wasn't very elegant, but I granted him the excuse of his youth. Brigitte was in tears and I was sincerely upset at her plight. She was my wife, but in a way she was also my daughter. However, I didn't want to take over the role previously played by her parents, so I told her she could go.

She packed, but then suddenly turned to me and said:
'I can't go this evening.'
'Why not?'
'It's the thirteenth.'
'You shouldn't be superstitious,' I told her. 'It's unlucky.'

The next day, on the set, she was acting the scene which we had just played out. According to the script, she had to burst into tears in the arms of her husband, played by Trintignant, because she was in love with another man. That evening she left the studio with Jean-Louis in his car. The roles had been reversed.

I lived in fear of the last day, the last shot, the last minute of filming. Fear of losing her altogether.

On 4 December 1956 . . . *Et Dieu créa la femme* had its première at the Normandie in the Champs-Élysées. Since then I have re-read my reviews with amusement. There are many contradictions, which is only to be expected. The attitudes taken by journalists vary according to regions, political views and countries. But I have noticed one remarkably persistent recurrent theme over the years: the critics never acknowledged that I had any talent at the time they wrote – they only admired my past work.

For instance, . . . *Et Dieu créa la femme* was badly reviewed, but quoted two years later as an example of non-conforming cinema. *Sait-on jamais*, which was again not very well received when it first came out, had become a film of ingenuous modernity to those who did not like *Les Liaisons Dangereuses* when it was first shown. The same cycle has been repeated from film to film, right up to the present day.

After the sarcasm with which it was greeted in Paris, . . . *Et Dieu créa la femme* received a triumphant welcome in the United States.

For the first time the Americans had been shown the female nude on the screen as a work of art, and they had been told that love for the pleasure of loving is not synonymous with sin. The Americans opened their eyes – and the market opened up for French films. Hollywood, which was sometimes licentious but always puritanical, didn't change overnight, but something irreversible had happened. Eight million Americans went to see my film and, although it was often mutilated by women's leagues and local censors, the Americans I meet today still remember it.

Much the same thing was going on in Lapland and Ecuador, in London and Diego Suarez. At a dinner a number of years later I found myself chatting with Jean Delmore, chairman of Air Liquide. 'Are you aware,' he said to me, 'that it was thanks to you that I was able to build my first liquid-oxygen plant in Japan?' I had not been aware. 'Columbia,' he went on, 'made several billion yen out of your film but they couldn't take it out of Japan. So they used the money to finance our plant.'

12.   America – Sinatra's way

Raoul Lévy's new idea appealed to me: a musical comedy with Brigitte Bardot and Frank Sinatra. However, as yet he only had a title – *Paris by Night*. We had been warned that Frank Sinatra was difficult – unless you were his friend – and that the only possible approach was to send a fully scripted screenplay to his agent. But information of this type never daunted Raoul. At midday he had mentioned the project to me. By six in the evening I had drafted three pages which we optimistically christened the summary of the screenplay. By midnight we had arranged an interview with Frank Sinatra in the Fontainebleau Hotel in Miami. The next morning we were in the plane.

Frank Sinatra got up at about four o'clock in the afternoon. He met us in his suite for the first whisky, dressed in bright orange lamé overalls and flanked by two curvaceous redheads who had stepped straight out of page one of a Peter Cheyney novel. His three bodyguards kept discreetly in the background. We didn't discuss the project, but contact was established and two hours later we had been adopted. Sinatra's humour concealed a character of cold steel tempered in the vicious struggles for survival he had fought on his way from the slums of Chicago to the mansions of California. The price of success had been to make him completely merciless, intolerant of both flattery and contradiction. The charm and appeal which made him irresistible were often lost behind the unpredictable whims of a spoilt child. He saw society as a jungle in which hunters and hunted rubbed shoulders and sometimes even walked a little way together.

However, he showed himself to be a perfect host in the

American manner and an agreeable friend. He invited us
to accompany him that evening to a dinner that was to be
given in a little Italian restaurant in honour of the engage-
ment of the owner's daughter. Spaghetti, chianti, songs
over the dessert, guitars and mandolins, it was very much
a family atmosphere.

After dinner we went back to the Fontainebleau for the
opening of a nightclub in which the fiancée's father and
Sinatra had business interests. Ella Fitzgerald was singing
there.

In James Hadley Chase's novels there is always a goddess standing at the bar whose eyes and hips would make
Venus blanch with jealousy. Her mysterious perfection is
generally compounded by the lure of danger. Well, she
was there too. In thirty seconds Raoul had succumbed to
this goddess, who, it transpired, had dreams of visiting
Paris. By three in the morning, madly in love, he had
placed his life and the French cinema at her feet.

By this time, the club was empty and Sinatra was
settling in for the night, surrounded by his bodyguards,
his bevy of girls and a few friends. Two men walked in –
silent, alert and menacing. The goddess turned a deathly
white and followed the men to the cloakroom. Through
the open door I saw a hand slap brutally across her face.
Her chinchilla coat was thrown over her shoulders and a
second later she had disappeared. It happened too quickly
for Raoul to react. Blissfully unaware of the danger or
reckless with passion, he rushed to the goddess's aid. It
was then that I had a chance to appreciate the professional
efficiency of Sinatra's bodyguards. When the two men had
walked in the first bodyguard had been at the back of the
room laughing and drinking. He had seemed to notice
nothing, but before Raoul had taken two paces he had
crossed the room, silently and without any superfluous
effort, and cut him off. With a grip like a vice he held
Raoul by the arm and forced him back to the bar.

'Drop it,' he said.

And as Raoul protested he added:

'D'you know who that was? She's the wife of . . .', and he mentioned the name of a famous boxing personality of the time.

He was in the process of getting a divorce, but the goddess still bore his name and his friends were not prepared to see her virtue tarnished. The champion didn't joke about matters of honour. Our bodyguard friend pointed out that it was only because Raoul was Sinatra's guest that he was not already on his way to hospital in an ambulance. He advised him not to push his luck any further.

We went back to our hotel. On some pretext which I do not remember Raoul asked me if I would not mind changing rooms. Unsuspectingly, I agreed.

Day was breaking when the door of my room (or rather Raoul's room) opened. Two men walked in and turned on the light. They opened the cupboards, glanced into the bathroom and left without a word.

At eight o'clock I was woken up again. This time by Raoul, who, looking nervous, told me that we were taking the first flight to Chicago.

'Why Chicago?' I asked.

'We have a meeting with Sinatra.'

'But Sinatra's here.'

'He'll be in Chicago as well.'

Raoul's logic was sometimes disconcerting. I insisted:

'Couldn't we just enjoy the sun for a bit? I'm fed up with flying.'

'Sinatra has invited us to the Basilio–Robinson fight. We can't miss the fight of the century.'

'But the fight isn't for three days yet.'

While talking, Raoul had packed in record time.

'I have my reasons,' he said. 'Get dressed quickly and meet me downstairs. I've had your case taken down already.'

Once in the plane, he relaxed and asked me if I had had a visit during the night.

'Yes,' I told him. 'Two men who were looking for something. They didn't say goodbye and I had to get up to turn off the light.'

'They were looking for the girl,' said Raoul. 'If I hadn't thought of swapping rooms with you I would be in the morgue or feeding the fish in Biscayne Bay by now.'

With suicidal recklessness he had invited his new friend to his hotel room and enjoyed three hours of ecstasy in her arms. Then, shortly before eight o'clock, she called to warn him that her chaperons had noticed her absence and that a swift departure was the only safe course. It was raining in Chicago. Mike Todd, the legendary producer with whom Raoul liked to compare himself, had just died in Mexico in a plane accident, and his widow, Elizabeth Taylor, was in the same hotel as us. We went to the funeral. Elizabeth Taylor, a tragic figure in black, barely able to walk, appeared to be in the deepest distress. Her sorrow excited the crowd. People clapped and wanted autographs. Her friends and the police had to protect her.

Frank Sinatra welcomed us in the royal suite on the top floor of the hotel and introduced us to the chief of police, with whom he was chatting. When we all left together for the fight we were accompanied by a motor-cycle escort, sirens blazing.

As Raoul had predicted, it was a great fight. Basilio poured with blood and Sugar Ray Robinson regained the world title on points after the full fifteen rounds. Afterwards, with the police chief still in tow, we had dinner in Cicero, the Chicago suburb where the gangsters had had their headquarters during the Prohibition era. A pilgrimage, in other words. The chief of police took a liking to me and apologized for the numerous cuts he had had made to . . . *Et Dieu créa la femme*, which was showing in the town at the time. It hadn't been out of prudery on his part, apparently, but a question of political realism. As I was now his friend, he swore to have the censored shots put back into the film.

He kept his word.

Frank Sinatra approved both the subject of *Paris by Night* and the part we had in mind for him. I started working on the screenplay with an American writer who had been chosen by mutual agreement, Harry Kurnitz.

As it turned out, the film was never made for a reason which had not occurred to either Raoul or me: Brigitte refused to work in Hollywood and Sinatra didn't want to work in Paris.

But I have never regretted making the trip.

13. Annette

They had blown up the gas stove inside their attic-room in the celebrated Hôtel des Ambassadeurs de Hollande, a classified ancient monument, and they had been turned out on to the street.

Both of them were blonde and they shared thirty-five summers almost equally between them. Annette gentle, sensual and capricious; Merete sparkling, vivacious, never still for a moment. They came from the north, but the sun followed them into any room. They knew twenty words of French – which they spoke with an indescribably barbaric accent – and fluent English. It was the Viking vanguard. For years to come Swedish, Norwegian, Finnish and Danish girls would descend in waves on Paris, invading the pages of fashion magazines and monopolizing eligible bachelors and faithless husbands alike. But none ever outshone this advance party, the Stroyberg sisters from Copenhagen.

When I first saw them I did not know that every single charmer in Paris was falling for them. Paul-Louis Weiller, always the first to know of events of this kind, had asked me to lunch. After the meal I picked up a book of humorous drawings by Jean Effel, *The Creation*, and translated the captions into English for the sisters, who laughed and leant their heads on my shoulders. The Devil was about to embark on another escapade – and more through laziness than any deliberate choice. The other book on the table was the second volume of the memoirs of Saint-Simon and a great deal harder to translate.

During the week that followed I saw Annette and Merete frequently. I was totally unable to make up my mind, and

I would certainly never have done it on my own. Fortunately, in affairs of the heart it is women who take the decisions, not men. One evening, in a discothèque in the rue Saint-Benoit, Annette decided that I was for her. She informed her sister of her decision and Merete renounced all claims with a good grace and, I hope, a pang of regret. My fate had been decided for me, and I hadn't the ghost of a chance of escaping it – not that I wanted to anyway.

By now I had been alone for four years. There had been difficult moments, but I had made a name for myself with the success of my first film, and it was only occasionally that I felt nostalgia for the time when I had been known as 'M. Bardot'.

I left for Venice to make *Sait-on jamais* with Robert Hossein, Christian Marquand, and Françoise Arnoul. Annette followed me there. Under grey skies, on freezing canals, in the cold of a Venetian January, she shone. She only had one evening dress, and she sold it on the sly to buy me a birthday present. The sweetness of loving and laughter replaced the turmoil of my relationship with Brigitte, and Annette came into my life through the wide-open door of happiness.

Back in Paris, I rented a small furnished studio in the avenue Montaigne. Annette bought dreadful doilies for the bedside tables, and changed the curtains. We had cream-cheese fights on the stairs. When summer came we migrated to Saint-Tropez. 'Chez Palmyre', where everyone danced the *galop* and the *java* to the strains of a barrel-organ and accordion, was still unspoilt. We had the great white beach at Pampelonne almost to ourselves. The dreadful crime Brigitte Bardot, Françoise Sagan and I had committed in making this little fishing port famous the world over had not yet taken its appalling toll. The day of retribution wasn't far off, but as yet we were blissfully ignorant. The papers were full of our extravagant spending sprees, scandals and debauchery. Our cha-cha-

cha sessions on the Esquinade and our pitched soda-bottle and syphon battles took on epic proportions when described by the press. And yet it was only the carefree uproarious abandon of children who refused to grow up despite being successful and almost thirty. We knew the world was changing, but when the alarm rings in the morning and you want to continue a pleasant dream, you close your eyes to have a few more minutes, and so did we. Françoise Sagan's royalties, although spectacular for a writer of her age, didn't in fact amount to a hundredth of the annual income of one of the really rich. Despite the aura of stardom that surrounded Brigitte Bardot, her life-style was in reality quite sensible, not to say modest. And as far as I was concerned, the four million old francs earned from *Sait-on jamais* had dried up long ago, and I was living on money allowed to me by Raoul Lévy in advance on my next film.

Annette was nicely pregnant while I was making *Les Bijoutiers du Clair de Lune* in Spain and on 6 December that year she gave birth to a seven-pound girl, Nathalie. Nathalie took her first steps at the end of the next summer, in the living-room of an old Provençal house surrounded by vines which I had rented in Saint-Tropez.

'How about getting married?' I said to Annette.

The Comte de Lausse, a one-time Foreign Legion officer, Commander of the Free French forces and mayor of the Lande des Maures area, heard our vows of eternal love and fidelity one sunny morning. All our friends were there. After the ceremony, under a hail of confetti, Annette clung tightly to my arm, looking radiantly happy. I led her to the car and helped her in beside me. An old woman leant towards me, grinning toothlessly.

'Heh, heh . . .' she chuckled. 'She's a pretty bride. But it won't last.'

'Why not?' I asked.

'Because you parked the car on the left-hand side of the town hall. That's a fatal omen. When the groom parks on the left-hand side the marriage never lasts; even in the old days, when there were carriages. Heh, heh, heh . . . it happened to me too. I was a widow two years after my wedding day. Heh, heh, heh . . .'

And off she went, apparently delighted with this old memory.

Annette seemed to be made for the traditional type of marriage, the kind where the husband works and keeps the family secure financially, and the wife looks after the house. Besides, we had a secretary, a nanny for our daughter, and a cook, so Annette had a lot of free time which she could spend travelling with me. The poor, put-upon *au pair* girl's dream had come true. And she had not had to buy it with years of work, or by marrying an old and ugly man for his money. I was thirty and I was more faithful than the average husband, despite the opportunities and temptations which abound in the life of a film director. Annette had killed two birds with one stone; she had love *and* security.

But, before long, even this was not enough – she wanted to work as well. I would have liked her to choose something where she could use her brain and gain a certain amount of independence. Instead, she chose the soft option – and decided to go into films. I advised her to go to drama school and learn the trade properly, but she wanted a big role right away. I was the only person who could give her one, so, like a good friend and husband, I forced her on my producer for the part of Mme de Tourvel in *Les Liaisons Dangereuses*. This gentle, reserved, faithful woman who yields to Valmont and goes insane could be played by an inexperienced actress, provided that the director took trouble to hide her weaknesses and managed to pass off her lack of professionalism as the shyness and awkwardness which the character demanded. I think I succeeded. The public loved Annette Vadim with her limpid blue eyes, her sensual, innocent body and the strange accent which made her seem so vulnerable. She held her own even when Gérard Philipe and Jeanne Moreau were on the screen.

While I was shooting the film in the Billancourt studios a young man with a stammer, shy and at the same time sure of himself, came to see me. He was going to make his first full-length film and wanted Annette to act in it. We found time between takes to chat in the canteen. If there had been a hole in the wall I think he would have dragged me into it. Before he went he left me the screenplay – one and a half erasure-covered pages, which I read carefully without understanding a word. This strange young man had impressed me, and I trusted him instinctively. I advised Annette to accept his offer. She refused. I pressed her, trying to make her understand that an actress must work, especially at the outset of her career. Even if it was a bad film she would at least have gained a little more experience. And if it was good (and I thought it might well be) she would have taken another step in her career. I failed to convince her. A pity, and her loss. The strange young man was called Jean-Luc Godard, and his film was *Breathless*.

The trials and tribulations of my film *Les Liaisons Dangereuses* began before we even started shooting. The knowledge that the best-known erotic novel in European literature (after de Sade, of course) was to be brought up to date and turned into a film simultaneously outraged the defenders of morality and sent academics reaching for their pens. Ever since the Renaissance writers have drawn inspiration from the classics and adapted them for the readers of their own day, but for the cinema to do the same was, it seemed, artistic high treason. A long trial ensued, brought about by the Society of Authors, which declared itself the responsible custodian of the French literary heritage, and hence the legitimate heir of Choderlos de Laclos. A lawyer called François Mitterand (who is now famous in a rather different field) pleaded the film director's cause successfully, won against an appeal, and finally won again in the High Court. This decision created a precedent which granted the cinema the freedom of inspiration it deserved.

Meanwhile, I had rather rashly agreed to let my wife act in the film. Annette found herself on the front cover of magazines the world over. 'After BB, the new Mme Vadim', proclaimed the headlines. This avalanche of publicity – which soon pushed all consideration of my writing and film-making into the background – took me completely by surprise. Naïvely, I had assumed that the 'press phenomenon' provoked by Brigitte's personality had been an exceptional case, unlikely to recur once we had gone our separate ways. But I was wrong. Overwhelmed by the consequences of my own imprudence, I had no option but to accept the situation. By contrast, my producer, Edmond Tenoudji, was delighted at all the free publicity, and congratulated himself for allowing me to put Annette in the film.

I was still looking for someone to play the part of the *ingénue*, Cecile de Volange. I found her on a beach in Nice. She came to Paris with her mother, and did a screen test. We liked what we saw, and Tenoudji signed her.

More cries of ecstasy from the press. Two weeks later, when the colour glossies came out there was a new name on everyone's lips: Gillian Hills. I now realized the extent to which Brigitte had influenced the press by starting the fashion for cinema 'discoveries'. But a few days before shooting began I discovered that Gillian had lied about her age and was not yet fifteen. I immediately spoke to my producer, and we agreed that it was too much of a risk to have a minor in the film. Poor Gillian. Her disappointment was a press editor's dream: the sad moral tale of the little girl from Nice who thought she was a star and found herself back behind a school desk was all over the papers.

The shooting of *Les Liaisons Dangereuses* drew to its close. In the penultimate scene the comtesse de Merteuil has to set fire to herself while trying to destroy some compromising letters. Despite her asbestos gown and the painstaking precautions we had taken, the young lady standing in for Jeanne Moreau was nearly burnt alive. Luckily, she escaped with only minor injuries, but it was a spectacular accident. I do not normally let reporters on to the set during takes because they tend to make a noise and sometimes even get so carried away that they move in front of the camera. However, on this occasion a photographer had slipped into the studio without my knowing it. He knew his job, and next day the photos of the accident were splashed across the front pages of several daily papers. Some of them ran the headline 'Jeanne Moreau nearly burned alive'. This sort of truth-twisting is common, and people generally think it has all been staged for publicity. Personally I have never gone in for that type of thing, though I must admit that there are others who don't have my scruples. They are, however, the exception rather than the rule.

When the film was finished it was submitted to the censors. They voted to ban it completely. Edmond Tenoudji and myself would have been happy to do without any additional publicity, but inevitably there was a good deal of talk about the decision, which was more or less unheard-of at the time, at least as far as French films were concerned. We appealed to the Minister of Information to lift the ban, and three days before the date we had planned for the première he agreed. Then on the morning of D-day we were informed that the Government had suspended the Minister's decision and had decided to hold an official viewing. De Gaulle had just returned to power, and moral conformity was the order of the day.

Things were looking black, Edmond Tenoudji was frantic and suggesting phoning all the guests to tell them the evening was off. I dissuaded him, as the Government Ministers were going to see the film that afternoon, and it was impossible to predict their decision. We might be lucky. (I omitted to mention that I had another, political, reason: if the Government decided to ban my film I was going to bring the whole affair into the open. I intended to fight repressive censorship, and this would be the perfect platform from which to start my campaign.)

At six p.m. we learnt that the official viewing was postponed until the evening, and that the doors of the cinema would remain closed. The political situation in Paris was fairly tense at that time, and large gatherings were forbidden. If the police were to start jostling and pushing back the six hundred guests we expected things might well turn nasty. I was stuck. On one hand, if the film were banned, ructions on the Champs-Élysées would be no bad thing, but, on the other hand, if the permit were granted it was likely that the film's opponents would use the disturbance to prolong their attack. I had already met Maurice Papon, the Parisian commissioner of police, and knew him to be a moderate man who liked the theatre and the cinema. I phoned his office and was lucky enough to get hold of him personally. He told me that he had been ordered to station his men in front of the cinema to stop anyone forcing their way in. However, he managed to allay my worst fears – the police would be in plain clothes.

It was a 'different' sort of première, to say the least. All Paris was there, waiting in the street. The doors of the cinema were locked, which showed that trouble was expected – normally a notice outside the box office would have been sufficient. However, the police in their raincoats stayed in the background and the evening passed off quietly. Meanwhile nine Ministers were doing me the honour of forgetting their political problems to follow the cynical exploits of Valmont and the comtesse de Merteuil. Apparently a heated debate ensued after the viewing, with the moderates emerging victorious. The film was authorized inside France for audiences over sixteen and was only prohibited from being exported, a ban which was lifted after three years anyway. What would our censors have thought if they had been told that fourteen years later the film would be shown on television to a family audience on a Sunday, and that no one would find the slightest cause for complaint?

Of course, next day all the papers were talking about the première of *Les Liaisons Dangereuses* which no one had managed to see. At the cost of a cold sweat Edmond Tenoudji had saved hundreds of thousands of francs on publicity.

14. Hesitation waltz to Tahiti

I adore the fantastic. Carmilla, the young vampire in Sheridan Le Fanu's novel, had always a special position in my own personal mythology. I decided to give her Annette's face. But, despite the success of my last film, persuading a producer and distributors to put their money into a film about a female vampire was no easy matter in an age of jet planes and television. It was madness, I was told, to take such a gamble when I had a hundred offers for so-called 'commercial' subjects with big stars. They were right, but I could imagine no better role for Annette, and I have never been very good at seeing reason. *Et mourir de plaisir* was a fine film, but ahead of its time.

Anyway, it gave its heroine a taste for freedom, not blood. It had been Annette's decision to use my name in the cinema, but now she saw it as an obstacle to the development of her personality. She could no longer bear to be thought of as someone's protégée. The young Stroyberg girl who once washed dishes to earn pocket money came out in revolt: she would owe nothing to anyone but herself. But I knew her career was as shaky as a house of cards. She had no particular gift for acting and only work and experience could save her from an abrupt return to reality. I had been her genie, covering up her weaknesses and giving her time to learn, but she believed in illusions and refused to admit that her success was only due to luck and good looks. Her laziness didn't help either. She was losing her head and confusing the overnight star with the real woman. People admired, flattered and wanted her too much, and she preferred to believe them rather than me. She suspected me of keeping her on a leash, of using her for my own ends. The director and the husband were plotting together to steal her life from her. I don't think she was fully aware of the turn her feelings had taken, but they were beginning to govern her behaviour.

It all began tritely enough, on a Riviera beach in the arms of a fashionable pop singer, good-looking in his way. He played the guitar, which completed the cliché. I found out several weeks later, and when I talked to Annette about it she said: 'I don't know what came over me' or 'it just happened' and 'I don't understand'.

She could never do anything about these things. Like many people without the capacity or the will to analyse themselves and face up to life, she thought that she was guided by Fate, that her destiny was beyond her control. She too succumbed to the first attack of happiness – like Brigitte, but for different reasons. She had been living out a fairy-tale and she believed in what her dreams promised her; reality was no longer enough. She would leave me, come back in tears, leave again, change her mind and swear she would stay with me for ever, then disappear again a week later.

The only constant during this chaotic period was a set of three dozen blue Murano glasses. They were tulip-shaped, like champagne glasses, and quite hideous, but Annette adored them. When she left home she would forget her fur coat or her passport, but never this set of blue glasses. If Annette wasn't in when I came home from work I would go straight to the kitchen. If the glasses were on the shelf it meant that all was well, and she had only gone to the cinema; if the shelf was empty, it meant she had gone to her lover.

Our hesitation waltz lasted six months. I did all I could to try and make things easier, hoping she was passing through a crisis period and that time was on our side. My main concern was for little Nathalie, who had just had her second birthday.

DENEUVE. 'Slender. her figure that of a shy and discreetly perverse adolescent straight out of a novel by Colette.'

Above: The director and the star of *La Vice et La Vertu* working together.

Right: of all the roles she played since her split with Vadim, Deneuve is best remembered as the elegant, masochistic heroine of Bunuel's *Belle de Jour.*

The making of a star. *Opposite, top left and right,* Catherine at 16 and 17; *Left:* with Vadim. Not even the birth of their son could keep them together.

Left: **FONDA**. 'Sweet, sensuous and full of laughter.'

Right: Jane and Vadim get married in Las Vegas.

Below: The conflict between Jane's role as a wife and mother and her growing need for political action grew intolerable during her years with Vadim.

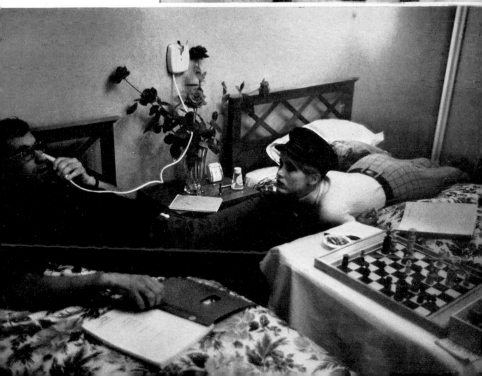

Right: The first of several films Jane made with Vadim was *La Ronde.* *Below:* As *Barbarella,* she plays the unprincipled heroine, ingenuously exploiting her sexuality. Jane hated the character and the part.

Above: The noble idea that destroyed a marriage. After her marriage had broken up, Jane made a controversial trip to North Vietnam at the height of the war.

Right: A family reunion as Vadim, Jane and their daughter Vanessa meet in 1971, two years after they had separated.

Above and left: 'He didn't do things the way everybody else did.' Away from the film set, Vadim with Vanessa and at work on *Memoirs of the Devil.*

Annette had a special knack of disappearing at the most inappropriate moments.

She began with a master stroke. I had just made *Et mourir de plaisir* for her. In a way it was her own film, her first really big part. The producers had organized a gala evening at Maxim's for the première. Annette was the star of the evening and seemed happy, surrounded by friends and the press, who had liked the film. Before the champagne sorbet she got up and left the table. I thought she had only gone for a couple of minutes, but she didn't come back. The cloakroom lady told me she had taken her coat. The vampire had vanished into thin air, leaving no message. She had answered her lover's call. I could just about understand that she lacked the courage to let me know, but not even to stay for the end of the evening, which had been intended as a present for her, and for which I had worked so hard – that was tactless. As I don't enjoy drinking when I am really depressed, I did not have the consolation that night of drowning my sorrows.

A few days later a repentant Annette slipped into our bed at dawn. Good tactics. By the time I had come to my senses, my gentle Viking had convinced me that she loved me, that she had wept every night and morning thinking about me, and that, of the two of us, it was she who had suffered more. She didn't understand what had happened to her and swore that from now on, all would be well.

I had just broken my ankle skiing, and was recovering from a difficult operation. Now I was to go into the operating theatre again to have the pin which had been holding the bones together removed. Less than a month after Annette's dawn appearance I was admitted to the Jouvenet Clinic. She came with me like a good wife, made sure I had things to read, put some flowers in the vases, kissed me tenderly and left with a radiant smile. Towards midnight, before the switchboard shut down, I rang the house. No reply. A merciful sleeping pill saved me from a night of worry.

E

Next day, before going into the operating theatre, I called home again. This time the nanny answered and gave me some surprising news: Annette had left for Saint-Tropez the day before. She had left me, smiling, with her night-train ticket already in her handbag. Her taste for pop music was becoming an obsession.

I came round from my anaesthetic with a headache and in a filthy mood. Claude Brulé, a very good friend of mine and a journalist on the *Paris-Presse*, came to see how I was.

'Are you in pain?' he asked.

'No, but I'm fed up.'

'How long before you're on your feet?'

'I don't know. But it won't be long before I get a divorce.'

Next day news of my divorce was on the front page of *Paris-Presse*, with a photo of Annette. That very evening the operator put a call through to me: 'It's your wife,' and I heard that inimitable Danish accent.

'I'm at Orly, darling. I'll be with you as soon as I can.'

She came into my room with the newspaper in her hand. She said she was sorry, wept a few dignified and discreet tears, and talked a lot about Nathalie. She explained that when she had seen the headline about the divorce the light had suddenly dawned. She had actually realized that she could not live without me. She did not know what had come over her. The singer meant nothing to her now – to prove it, she hadn't even told him she was leaving him. I pointed out that that argument works both ways, but she maintained I did not understand at all. I was at a disadvantage – I could not even walk her to the door. So I let her stay the night in the armchair.

Days passed, and then weeks. Annette was still with me. Life began again as before, despite some worrying moments of depression. I took the view that our hearts would heal more easily in Paradise than Paris, so I decided to take her to Tahiti with me. I had previously persuaded the Paramount bosses to send me to the Pacific islands to look for locations for a film I wanted to make.

We flew to Hollywood, where I sorted out the financial problems with the studio, and then on to Honolulu. We kissed civilization goodbye on board a Constellation, joyfully celebrated 'crossing the line' with some of the passengers and crew, and landed at Bora Bora as drunk as lords. A little seaplane was waiting for us on the deep green waters of the lagoon to take us on the last leg of the journey. By the time we reached Papeete Bay we were in a state of absolute collapse.

The postcards were right – Tahiti before the French nuclear tests and their fall-out of soldiers and civil servants did look like Paradise – a Paradise where there was laughter and song instead of prayers, and love instead of eternity. I was immediately struck by the islanders' attitude to money. They acknowledged its usefulness, but no one lived for it. But this innocence could not last. Soon people would come to create needs and inequality, buy the smiles and the singing and – their supreme achievement – offer the gentle Tahitians class-consciousness and politics. Today, under the breadfruit and coconut trees, you are a Gaullist or a Marxist, you vote for Mitterand or Giscard d'Estaing, you are afraid of the future, and everything is as it should be.

In 1961 Tahiti was living out its last moments of true freedom. Pleasure was the only moral code. In the villages, the children regarded every house as their home. The older mothers brought up their neighbours' children with just as much care as their own, leaving the younger wives time to have fun. Tahitian women divided men into two categories: young and old. Old meant over twenty. After that it made no difference if one was thirty or sixty. It was natural and even common to find an eighteen-year-old girl living with a man three times her age. She would sometimes go to the beach at night to have a good time with a 'young' man, and the arrangement passed off perfectly happily. Problems of heating, transport and dress were unheard-of, and no one envied the few shop-keepers and ship fitters on the island who had become rich. Money brought nothing but worry and extra work; and to them work was at best a necessary evil, to be reduced to a strict minimum.

When I arrived in Papeete the prison housed only one occupant. The warder drove him in a jeep every morning to clear some land for cultivation and then went to sleep in the shade of a tree. The prisoner woke him up when it was time to go back. One day a coconut fell on the guard's head and he did not wake up. The prisoner had to put him in the jeep and drive him back to the prison. This sort of story was very popular and would form the main topic of conversation for days. The only problem was alcohol. The Tahitians loved drinking, but couldn't quite cope with it. By the third glass they would become violent and brawls broke out every evening in Papeete's one nightclub. But the real celebrations took place on the beaches. There they danced the *tamoure*, sang and gossiped – the women would hold forth in detail about their own and other people's amorous adventures. They adored Annette with her blue eyes, blonde hair and loved her for her kindness. Even when I returned to Papeete some years later they were still talking about her.

I had rented a boat to go round the Tua Motu atolls. I needed a captain, and the Governor offered to lend me his. His name was Mami, and his dazzling blond hair (in all other respects he was a Tahitian through and through) had earned him tremendous success with the ladies of Papeete. Despite his youth he had just reached his twelfth wife, but he was a good father and visited his ex-wives regularly every Sunday, bundling his children into an old convertible Peugeot, and taking them for a drive along the twelve miles of car-worthy road on the island.

For my trip I had chosen a sturdy old Pacific two-master built at the turn of the century in Panama. I felt like a character in a story by Robert Louis Stevenson. Mami knew all the atolls and their secrets. The lagoons inside their green and white rings, lost in the faded sky and the dark blue sea, struck me as even more beautiful than the miraculous landscape of the Windward Islands.

This land of pleasure and informality where everyone was on Christian name terms suited me perfectly. I thought about that other universe where happiness can be had at a price – but one which takes all the pleasure out of it. Annette let the magic of the islands wash over her, but I felt that she was missing France already. We returned via New York and reached Orly early one morning. Our friends were impatient to hear our news and that night found us all in a Spanish restaurant in the rue Gît-le-Cœur. After the paella Annette got up and left the table. I thought she had only gone for a couple of minutes; I was facing the wall and didn't see her leave. When she didn't come back, my friends asked me where she had gone. Christian Marquand had already guessed what was happening and answered for me.

'She likes French love songs better than the *tamoure*.'

Annette's abrupt departures were beginning to get on my nerves.

She made a few more attempts to start her life with me again. But I decided to suffer bravely, and refused to play her game any more. The hardest thing about breaking-up isn't the end of the love affair, but the realization that part of oneself leaves with the other person. It is very much an operation carried out without anaesthetic.

The singer didn't last and Annette continued migrating southwards. She believed the golden promises of the Italian producers and went to live in Rome. She was welcomed as a big star, hounded by the *paparazzi*, and propositioned by famous actors. However, Italians turn off as fast as they turn on. A few months later she had made one film of little interest, which came and went unnoticed and marked the end of her career. It was a waste and it saddened me. Even if I occasionally entertain the idea of vengeance, I get no pleasure from seeing it carried out. And Annette had left me a priceless gift – our little daughter.

Women rightly complain about their low pay and of being treated as objects of male desire, but they always forget that the greatest injustice in our society works in their favour: the right to keep their children. I know they give birth to them, but can life really be reduced to an owner's rights to his property? Do nine months of discomfort and a few hours' intense pain endow a human being with a deed of ownership? The law which states that in all circumstances a child must belong to its mother is absurd and I know many children who have suffered as a result of it. Court decisions which go that way are sometimes just, but they should not be automatic.

Although Nathalie was only two, Annette knew I was fully able to bring her up. She didn't want to expose her to the hazards of an existence which might well be too insecure and unstable. When she made her decision she was certainly wiser than any judge would have been, and I have always been grateful to her for it.

Today Nathalie is eighteen. She is healthy, has chosen a career she loves. She says she is happy and as her friends tell me the same thing, I have no reason to doubt it.

Annette went through the bad years courageously. She has married again and now has two other children. I hope she is happy, and that she has lost her habit of disappearing during meals.

15. Catherine Deneuve

Sometimes in moments of melancholy, or when I'm day-dreaming, I play a game that I call 'life transfers'. I think of a woman or a man whom I have known intimately. I reconstitute a portrait of that person at the time when I knew them. When the picture is clear I view it in juxta-position with the image of the person as he or she is today. The results are always fascinating, and sometimes un-believable. The greater the contrast, the more successful the game. Number 1 in my 'life transfer' hit parade is Catherine Deneuve.

You all know Catherine, with her long, light yellow hair, her sensitive but severe face, her rather stiffly held figure, her impeccable make-up. She is the archetype of the elegant, romantic young woman so beloved by the French cinema. Playing the tart in *Zig-Zag*, she looks uncomfortably out of character; but when she lends her pure, glacial face to one of Bunuel's heroines, she comes close to perfection. If you didn't know her photograph from the newspapers and you met her crossing a street in Paris, you'd think that she was a young, wealthy middle-class girl from the snobbish *seizième arrondissement*.

1962: her hair is dark chestnut, shoulder length. She is slender, her figure that of a shy and discreetly perverse adolescent straight out of a novel by Colette. The evening I first met her she was dancing the Charleston, which had just come back into fashion – and there was I, twice disappointed in love, convinced that women were stronger and more cynical than men, wary of anything that might hurt me. I tried to love her, but I was passing through a temporary crisis of misogyny and although I'm a naturally affectionate person I was sometimes cruel. She put up with the good times and the bad times with apparent serenity – I never noticed that she was sharpening her claws in silence. Eventually we decided to get married. The wedding was to be celebrated in Tahiti, where my friend Paul Gégauff was shooting a film that I had promised to supervise.

We stopped over in New York to settle some matter or other with my impresario. And it was in New York, at the Hotel Sherry Netherland, that I received an unexpected telephone call from Annette.

'If you marry that girl,' she said, 'I will take Nathalie back.'

It was straightforward, clear-cut – and, naturally, 'for my own good'. I did not dare risk calling her bluff and I decided to postpone the wedding. Catherine appeared to understand my attitude, but I believe that something changed in her that day.

On our return from Tahiti three events occurred almost at the same time, events which were to transform the shy young girl profoundly. She bleached her hair, which she now wore long; she moved into another flat which she proceeded to furnish and decorate like an experienced housewife; and she decided to go into films.

This sudden urge to enter the world of films took me by surprise. Catherine had always maintained that she did not want to follow in the footsteps of her older sister, Françoise Dorléac, whose career as a young leading actress had started with a bang. Was it modesty or pride? I never knew. Catherine had played a very minor part at the age of fourteen in a film starring Françoise, called *Les portes claquent*. It was just a giggle, she had told me, and I believed her. Her true career in the cinema started with me, in *Le Vice et la Vertu*. She was Virtue, martyred by Vice (Annie Girardot and Robert Hossein), but emerging victorious and spiritually intact from the experience. A moral tale, obviously.

Soon my shy adolescent had blossomed out into a hard-headed woman ruthlessly in control of her life. I couldn't get used to this new personality. She became peremptory and bossy, and that was something I couldn't accept. The birth of a little boy did not bring about the miracle of reconciliation for which we both hoped. My experience has taught me to believe that the arrival of a child never rescues a relationship that's in trouble. On the contrary – the joys of motherhood are often accompanied by irrational anxieties and unreasonable pessimism. Moreover, there is nothing worse for a child than to grow up in an atmosphere of instability or hatred: if the parents separate at least it's easier to pretend that they still love each other. To stay together when nothing is going right has never solved the children's problems, at least in today's society.

No doubt this sketchy description of my relationship with Catherine simplifies – and even falsifies – the truth. The subject really demands a full-length novel. But it isn't easy to condense into a few sentences all the tenderness, passion, disappointment, the hope, bitterness and exhaustion that make up a relationship one has lived through.

I admit that I share a good deal of the blame for this episode. In particular I was afraid of Annette. The idea that she might take Nathalie back terrified me and no doubt I took the easy way out by giving in to her. It looked as if I still cared for her. It wasn't the case at all, of course, but how could I prove it?

Today Catherine Deneuve is rich, she loves and is loved. She has won her place among the stars.

What you might call a fairy story, isn't it?

16. 'Miss Fonda will never film with Roger Vadim'

It was a summer's day. A fact hardly worth mentioning in southern California, where seasons exist only in the calendar and summer never dies. The single-storey house with its ivy-covered roof faced on to the Pacific Ocean to the west, with a little garden on its eastern side. I was standing in front of the whitewood porch in jeans and bare feet with my baby in my arms. Vanessa, fourteen months old, chubby and suntanned, was proudly wearing her plastic pants over her nappy. Her entire vocabulary consisted of four words, which she spoke in a low, slightly broken voice, like an old actress or a meths-drinking tramp. She waved to her Mummy, who was going off to war.

Jane Fonda, armed with Nikon and tape recorder, made a fine figure in her leather jacket. Next to her stood her loyal lieutenant, Elisabeth Vailland, a little martial mouse. They were going off together to the front – the university campuses and the military barracks – to do battle for peace in Vietnam. Their exploit was a daring one and at that time (November 1969) they were running a real risk. America was discovering political awareness through violence, fanaticism and disorder, and their chances of landing in prison or hospital were more than theoretical. Jane, upset at having to leave her daughter, was holding back her tears like a true soldier. I was worried for her and the fact that we had decided to separate a few months earlier did not alleviate my anxiety. Only Elisabeth's presence did anything to reassure me. Twenty years of living with Roger Vailland had given her experience of politics and men that Jane had not yet acquired, and I hoped that she would be a good adviser.

With my child in my arms, I once more urged Jane to take care as she sat in the driver's seat and switched on the engine. Suddenly I heard shouts of laughter from Christian Marquand, who had been watching the scene. I asked him what it was he found so funny. Between hiccups he told me it was a real joy to see the world turned upside down: the wife going off to war and the husband staying at home to feed and look after the children. It was enough to make Colonel Blimp turn in his grave.

My break-up with Jane Fonda was attracting plenty of comments in the press, all of them contradictory. On the one hand, Jane was seen as the symbol of enslaved woman freeing herself from the yoke of marriage. The woman who had been exploited at work by her director husband and condemned by the same tyrant to run a house, receive his friends and produce children, was courageously rejecting her traditional subjection. On the other hand, I was reputed to be a kind of Svengali who had opened the doors of life and politics to his wife, but who had been unable to hold her back when she was fired with inspiration.

The truth is more subtle and, perhaps, rather more interesting. To understand, we must go right back to the beginning.

I feel like starting with the telegram.

A friend of mine, the producer Francis Cosnes, was planning to adapt *Angélique, la marquise des Anges*, a best-seller of the 1960s, for the cinema. He suggested that I direct the film, with Jane Fonda as Angélique. I only knew Jane (whose main claim to fame was that she was Henry Fonda's daughter) from photographs; in make-up and a Hollywood hairstyle she looked quite pretty, but odourless and insipid. Nevertheless, I sensed that behind the directness of her eyes, behind the aggressive, athletic stance of her body, lay something else – a troubled, fascinating personality. I approved Francis Cosnes'

choice and he contacted Jane's agent. We did not have to
wait long for the terse cabled reply: 'Miss Fonda will
never film with Roger Vadim.' I learned the reason for
this refusal later. Jane had believed in my reputation as a
cynical, debauched ogre lusting after virgin flesh, a
diabolical magician who, unlike the alchemists, trans-
formed precious metal into lead, roses into thistles. The
fact that she changed her mind at our first meeting is
doubtless because she found a human being as different
from his legend as day from night. My faults were not
those she expected and my qualities took her by surprise.

One year after the telegram I was preparing a remake of
La Ronde with a screenplay by Jean Anouilh. The Hakim
brothers, my producers, wanted Jane Fonda for the part
of the unfaithful young woman. I told them she was
bound to refuse.

'You can never be sure with actors,' Robert Hakim
told me.

He was right: Jane was shooting a film by René Clément
in France and had just met one of my friends. They had
talked about me and, curious to know what I was really
like, she agreed to meet me at dinner at the home of her
agent, Olga Horstig.

For the second time in my life I was to be the victim of
that strange disease, love at first sight. Nobody knows
what causes it and the scientific explanation for its fatal
effects is still a mystery. So far mankind has been unable
to come up with an antidote. It is far more dangerous
than flu or whooping cough, but, at least in my experience,
infinitely more agreeable. There is no incubation period.
From the appearance of first symptoms – three to ten
seconds after direct contamination – you know you are
doomed. Some people turn into absolute fools, others
become outstandingly brilliant. Blind optimism alternates
with unreasoning anxiety. If you are suffering from
rheumatism, stomach-ache, corns or chronic neuralgia,
all your pain disappears in the presence of the object of

adoration – only to start up again with renewed ferocity as soon as that object moves more than ten yards away. In most cases your sexual powers melt away without warning at the most inopportune moment. If, after this fatal experience, you manage to resist your immediate impulse to leap out of the window, you become an indefatigable lover for the duration of the disease.

What happens after the attack subsides follows no known law. It ranges from a brutal awakening in a gloomy, hostile world to eternal love. Also, one should distinguish between the bilateral and unilateral versions of the disease. The victim of the latter, alone gripped by the paralysing virus, lapses into madness and amorous megalomania. Nothing deters him, neither bald facts, nor logic, nor humiliation. His convalescence is long and painful. The victim of the bilateral form of the disease, on the other hand, seems to be in a privileged position. Since double megalomania exists only in love, its effects are limited, though terrifying. But he manages to avoid madness, since his partner in fantasy is real. It is waking up which is the difficult part. You can't forget a dream shared by two. It pursues the couple, haunts them, colours their lives for ever. It is the gold standard, the diamond against which each moment of life is judged.

Jane left Olga Horstig's flat at about one in the morning. As soon as she got back to her hotel room, she telephoned to say that she would act in my film. The attraction that had drawn us to each other from the very first moment of meeting was so obvious that Olga, amused and surprised, laughed up her sleeve. And yet Jane avoided me over the next few days. She was still afraid. Then we ran into each other at Eddie Barclay's annual fancy-dress ball at the Pavillon d'Armenonville. She was dressed as Charlie Chaplin and I was wearing the uniform of an officer in the Soviet army. All night long we weaved around each other, the clown seeking out and then rebuffing the soldier, the soldier at a loss but nevertheless certain that he would win through in the end. As dawn broke, she disappeared.

Some time later (I find it difficult to account for those days) I went to the Épinay studios where Jane was filming with Alain Delon. I had an appointment with Jean André, the set designer who had worked on almost all my films.

Jean and I sat and chatted at a table in the studio canteen. Somebody told Jane that I was there. I saw the door open and Jane, out of breath, wearing a raincoat she hadn't bothered to button, ran into the room. She stopped short in embarrassment at betraying her emotions, and then walked towards us. Her breast was heaving, her hair – just arranged by the studio stylist – was wet and disarranged, her face was flushed beneath the make-up. She looked beautiful and sensitive and vulnerable and divine. That evening we returned from Épinay to Paris together so that we would not have to part . . . I was going to say 'so that we would never have to part'.

Fate organized my life like an old nanny who shoos away unwanted visitors on the wedding night of the child she has cherished. Catherine Deneuve had left a few weeks earlier to live for a trial period with a famous singer (I seem to be dogged by guitarists!). Annette Stroyberg, overcome by a sudden burst of maternal feeling (or perhaps because she had been disappointed by Italy), had asked me to find her a flat in Paris so that she could live there with her daughter. Consequently, I was absolutely free for the first time in years. It is difficult to describe happiness, and anyway it isn't a subject that interests other people, so I will skate over the weeks of happiness which Jane and I lived through in our tiny flat in the rue Séguier, near the Seine. In the morning we would leave for the studios at Saint-Maurice where I was filming *La Ronde*. On non-working days we might decide to jump on a train or an aeroplane and wander round Amsterdam or along a beach in Finistère.

I can't remember how the idea of the trip to Russia arose. Jane wanted to see the country about which people in the United States told such awful stories and, as far as I was concerned, the idea of a pilgrimage to the kingdom of my forefathers had always tempted me. We managed to get visas without difficulty and one morning we took off from Le Bourget in a gigantic Ilyushin turbo-jet which looked more like a transatlantic liner or the Orient Express than an aircraft.

On our arrival in Moscow we were given a room on the fifth floor of the National Hotel. From the balcony which overlooked the Gorki Prospect we had a grandstand view of the last-minute preparations for the May Day festivities. At about midnight we were woken by a terrifying noise. We went out on to the balcony. The whole of the avenue had been invaded by strange primeval creatures, some of them as high as the third floor of our hotel. They were covered with immense grey tarpaulins and seemed to have materialized out of thin air, like prehistoric monsters spewed out by some infernal time machine. I recognized the scraping sound of their caterpillar tracks, the growl of tank and transporter engines, the high-pitched stammer of motor-cycles riding beside the columns. I remembered Toulon and the roads of Normandy with a spasm of nervous excitement. Jane, who had turned as white as a sheet, was too shocked to speak. For the first time the idea of war had come home to her as a reality. She moved away from the window and threw herself on the bed with her head buried in her arms. I wondered whether she was going to have an attack of hysteria, faint or merely vomit. It took me a long time to calm her down. I explained that the Russian army was simply positioning itself for the next day's parade, but until five o'clock in the morning the noise of death and madness made the walls of our room tremble. Only at dawn did Jane manage to sleep.

At about ten the next morning we stood watching the parade from a balcony overlooking Red Square. It was an impressive display and one could feel an almost physical sensation of implacable, inhuman strength. By comparison, the Bastille Day parade down the Champs-Élysées seemed like a march of toy soldiers. Nevertheless, this display of machines for killing was less shattering than the previous night's hallucinatory vision. Now I could see the giants without their grey tarpaulins – nuclear missiles glinting in the sun before an awestruck public.

But after death came life: the peoples of all the Soviet Socialist Republics, preceded by musicians and followed by dancers, invaded Red Square in their gaily coloured costumes. They made a river of colour and joy, filling the celebrations with love and hope. Fathers carried children on their shoulders, girls scattered smiles everywhere – and the crowd applauded with far greater enthusiasm than it had shown for the tanks and missiles.

'It looks like a hippy holiday,' Jane said to me. She was beginning to love the Russians.

Despite what we had been told (that the Russians are surly and badly dressed), we were struck mainly by their good humour and simplicity during our visit. The people dressed in an unstudied, unrefined way, but what is functional is not necessarily ugly. With the exception of the appalling hats worn by some of the officials' wives nothing shocked me.

One day in Leningrad, however, we did see a group of people who were horribly dressed and looked unkempt and vulgar. I was on the point of revising my opinion when I realized that they were foreign tourists.

Intourist had made a young student called Tania available to act as our interpreter. In fact we didn't really need her, since a woman friend who spoke Russian fluently had come with us from Paris, and during the first week we used Tania's services only rarely. She was intelligent, discriminating and not without a sense of humour (Russian humour is very special and most foreigners do not understand it). We struck up a friendship with her and towards the end of our stay we became inseparable. She introduced us to the world of young intellectuals, whom the tourists and politicians visiting Russia never get the opportunity to meet.

These boys and girls knew far more about politics and life in the capitalist world than I imagined. They lacked news and opportunities to travel (although some of them had been to France), but they didn't seem to want to change their own regime. Their main complaint seemed to be the sluggishness of the Russian bureaucracy, a curse which they did not attribute solely to the Communist apparatus, but also to a congenital flaw in the Russian mentality. 'It was just the same in the time of the Tsars,' they used to say. 'Even then you needed a pass to travel from one town to another.'

In 1965 destalinization was in full swing and Khrushchev was in power. A liberalizing wind of change was blowing, and any hope was permissible. Today the standard of living has risen, the housing problem is less acute, but censorship has once again become more stringent. Nevertheless, everything that I saw and heard during that month of May gave me the feeling that young Russians are capable of building a truly Communist society. They want to live their own revolution instead of having it imposed upon them like irresponsible children. Perhaps Khrushchev made mistakes in the economic field and I'm not qualified to judge the effects of his foreign policy, but I think it's a pity for the future of his country that he was disposed of so soon.

The main targets for the irony of the Soviet citizen were the petty officials, followed closely by the Chinese. In general, they expressed an almost sentimental attachment to the French, a great deal of interest in and admiration for the American people, and cordial hatred of their oriental neighbours. One evening we went to the theatre to see *Princess Tirando*, a musical comedy which is part of their standard repertory. One scene was set in the court

Imagine a mile or more of white sand. To one side, the Pacific – a lazy ocean, breathing slowly and regularly as if to conceal its own massive strength. To the other, a friendly wall of houses, each in a style of its own: Spanish, northern French, chalet-style or English – some of them modern and built all in glass, but most made of wood. Two or three of them, the oldest, are giants of three storeys. In the haze, twenty miles to the south, is the port of Los Angeles. At weekends a hundred or so children and about the same number of grown-ups run about on the sand and plunge shrieking into the icy breakers. There is a current coming from Alaska, and the water is seldom warm. During the week the beach belongs to the dogs. A few fishermen cast their lines, sometimes fifty yards or more in length, depending on how good they are and the kind of rod they have. From time to time a solitary nature-lover walks along the water's edge, escorted by the dogs, who take it in turns to dash past him barking. After school the children from the houses along the beach emerge, and at sunset pairs of lovers make their appearance.

About three hundred yards away, back from the beach and just in front of a line of hills, runs the Pacific Coast Highway. Here, scattered higgledy-piggledy, like an unfinished building project, are the supermarket, the veterinary clinic, the bank, the mini-hospital, the mini-fire station and the post office. Less than ten miles away, in Beverly Hills, where the rich Hollywood people live, you get arrested by the police if you go on foot in the streets, but in Malibu you can live all the year round without putting shoes on. This was the unexpected paradise to which Jane had brought me for our first stay in California.

At that time she did not think it was a betrayal of womanhood to be a housewife, and in spite of her career as an actress she was in fact an extremely good one. I used to let her get on with it, because I thought it was what she liked. And so she did, I believe, though a few years later she would refer with self-righteous indignation to her 'housewife' period. I should have been very happy myself to be in a caravan, but this dream existence she created for me to live was even more agreeable, and I saw no reason to turn it down. If I had realized, I should certainly have done something about it, as it was Jane I loved, much more than a comfortable life and good cooking.

I divided my time between fishing, writing the script of *La Curée* and playing host to friends. But the most enjoyable moments were those I spent with Jane, either in the daytime or at night. My daughter Nathalie was going to school on the other side of the Highway, up on the hill, and spent her free time on the beach or in front of the television set. In America children are not given homework, but this doesn't seem to prevent them from passing their exams, when the time comes, just as well as French children.

In August the black population of Watts in the heart of Los Angeles took to the streets and began burning and looting anything they could lay their hands on. I was not watching television that particular morning, and on my deserted beach had no idea that anything was wrong. We had a black cook who came into Malibu by car every day from her place in Watts. The car was always breaking down, so I wasn't surprised when she rang up and asked me to come and fetch her.

I had rented an old but roomy Ford convertible which I used to leave, unlocked, in the street – where it never managed to attract the slightest interest from even the most amateur car-thief. I called it my bath-tub and with good reason. Driving in California, with its speed limits, its traffic lights and its three- or four-lane freeways, is

virtually a matter of remote control. You take your place
at the steering wheel as if you are getting into your bath,
and if nothing unforeseen happens you come to when you
reach your destination. If there is an accident, the result is
indescribable confusion, because drivers have become
conditioned over the years to never having to take any
initiative. (The same malady has recently begun to appear
in France.) But on this particular day I was going to have
a chance to show my virtuosity as a driver. The experience
I had gained during the years I had gone in for racing
Ferraris was fortunately not entirely wasted.

I was just coming into Santa Monica, day-dreaming at
forty-five miles an hour on the Pacific Coast Highway,
when I noticed a mushroom of smoke rising up from the
centre of Los Angeles. I threaded my way through the
police cars and ambulances towards the fire, which I
realized was in the black district. Heavy machine-guns
were in position at the crossroads, and a few tanks were
manoeuvring clumsily in the streets. I wondered vaguely
what on earth they were doing there. There was the
crackle of gunfire, and the sound of explosions punctuated
the incessant screaming and wailing of sirens. There was so
much confusion that nobody attempted to stop me.

I found Martha, my cook, sitting on the pavement in
front of her house, surrounded by piles of wreckage.

'Has your car broken down?' I asked her.

'I think it's burnt out,' said Martha.

'You didn't tell me about these fun and games on the
phone.'

'I forgot to send you a free ticket,' replied Martha, who
wasn't easily shaken. 'Didn't they ask you for it when you
came in?'

'I managed to gatecrash,' I said.

She asked me if I would mind taking her children to
Malibu, as the school was closed.

'Those intellectuals' – she meant the schoolteachers –
'never miss the chance of taking some time off.'

I agreed to take the children. She turned towards the inside of the building and waved, and within a matter of seconds my car was invaded by a horde of kids ranging from eighteen months to fourteen years old.

Crossing into Switzerland under the nose of the Germans was one thing, getting out of Watts with its invasion force of American troops and police was quite another. I bounced from one pavement to the other, charged headlong through clouds of smoke, zigzagged round tanks. Bullets were whistling through the air, so the children told me later, but I was concentrating too hard on what I was doing to bother about little details of that sort. After what seemed like an eternity we managed to get through, and finally arrived at Malibu without any further trouble. Twelve little black urchins, boys and girls, poured out of every corner of the car, including the boot, and rushed through the house down to the beach. I congratulated Martha on her numerous family and she admitted that only two of them were hers. Most of the children were running about on the beach for the first time in their lives. They were uttering loud shrieks, which my cook assured me were only shrieks of joy.

The residents of Malibu are a very mixed lot when it comes to social background and political opinion. They include writers, painters, actors, millionaires, shop-keepers, the conventional middle class and some of the traditionally wealthy Californian families. Bohemia lives next door to Mammon, anarchy to stern morality. Malibu is like a common waterhole in Africa, where the game come down to drink from the same source, carnivores and herbivores together, and for a short hour behave like brothers.

However, the explosion in Watts had stirred up class reactions and latent racism. Some of my neighbours were convinced that the D-day of black revolution (organized by the Communists and the Black Panthers) had dawned. The members of the extreme right-wing John Birch

Society mistook the children for an assault commando and telephoned the Sheriff to say that the blacks were occupying Malibu. Ten minutes later, all the cars from the local police station had converged on my house. The Sheriff and his men burst in, revolvers at the ready, in the best Hollywood tradition. After a lot of hard talking they agreed to let me keep the children until Watts returned to normal, on condition that I didn't let them leave the house.

For them the bathing season hadn't lasted long.

Jane was shooting, and only saw what happened at Watts on the television news. But she had other opportunities of seeing the impact of the black problem on the United States. On one occasion Otto Preminger was directing *Hurry Sundown* on location in Louisiana. The company was staying in a motel at Baton Rouge, the State capital, which is in the heart of the traditional South. The cast included Jane Fonda, Michael Caine, Faye Dunaway and John Philip Law, but there were a number of black actors too. When it was heard that they were all using the same swimming pool the producers were threatened with assassination, and the Ku Klux Klan gave notice that the 'niggers' were to be moved immediately to another hotel. After a hurried meeting the actors unanimously decided that they would stop shooting if the producers gave in to these threats, so four armed policemen took turns to mount a day and night watch on the hotel. It was a strange feeling to be bathing in the pool in broad daylight surrounded by guards pacing up and down on the first-floor terrace: just like being in Sing Sing, in fact.

Much of the action in the film took place in a large house looking like something out of *Gone with the Wind*. Nothing seemed to have changed since before the Civil War. Then one day the company moved off to do some shooting in a small town nearby.

Jane, who had a few moments to herself, was walking with me along the street. A little black boy of seven or eight gave her a flower, and she bent down to kiss him. Then something very strange happened. People stopped and stared at us in silence. The atmosphere in the street, which only a moment ago had seemed happy and full of life, suddenly became ominous and uncomfortable, full of unspoken threats. Claude Azoulay, a *Paris-Match* reporter who had just taken a picture of the scene, was the first to sense the change.

'They don't seem to like you kissing blacks,' he said to Jane.

She burst out laughing.

'Don't be silly,' she said, 'he's only a child.'

An hour later the Sheriff suddenly appeared right in front of Otto Preminger's camera, and Preminger, taking him for an actor, began to bellow at him in a fury. The Sheriff wasn't impressed, however, and informed him that the whole team were to leave town immediately. He said he couldn't guarantee their safety for more than half an hour. As we drove out two of our windscreens were holed by bullets, which could easily have killed the drivers or passengers.

Jane's kiss cost Paramount the equivalent of a whole day's shooting – a good sixty thousand dollars.

Jane's subsequent campaigns on behalf of the Indians or the blacks have looked like publicity stunts to some Europeans who don't fully understand the acuteness of the racial problem in the United States and of the violence it produces. But they shouldn't confuse her convictions with their own ignorance: seeing a Negro lynched in the cinema and seeing it in real life are two very different experiences.

Between Watts and Baton Rouge Jane and I had spent forty-eight hours at the Dunes Palace in Las Vegas. Not to play roulette or blackjack. To get married.

18. Barbarella versus Women's Lib

I got on marvellously with Jane on the set. She was disciplined and professional, she always concentrated on her work, and she showed all the qualities of English-speaking actors and actresses without losing any of her basic niceness and spontaneity. And she never took unfair advantage of the director on set by exploiting her femininity. I wish I could say the same of all the actresses I have worked with.

When shooting for *La Curée* ('The Quarry') first started, she was a bit disconcerted by the way I handled the actors. By talking and creating a certain atmosphere on the set before I begin filming I help an actor to get inside the skin of the character he is playing, sometimes without him realizing it. If I don't like the result, then, and only then, do I start giving specific directions. But I prefer the other method.

I told Jane that really good actors, because of their technique and their temperament, *give* themselves to the character they are playing. Stars merely *lend* themselves to the character: their personality is so strong that it always retains its own colouring. If Laurence Olivier, for instance, plays Richard III he *becomes* the king – cruel, passionate, and Machiavellian. If Marlon Brando plays the same part Richard III will become Brando. Rhett Butler *is* Clark Gable, Mister Deeds *is* Gary Cooper. Jane thought she had no personality, and was desperately searching for an identity for herself. In front of the camera she analysed herself constantly, buried herself in introspection, and tried to find a justification for every word, every movement and every smile. She was basically afraid of herself. This lack of self-esteem was her greatest weakness. She thought that through hard work she could 'fabricate' a talent for herself, but refused to admit that she already had something unique, infinitely rarer and more precious than courage and will-power. Her sense of justice led her to believe that everyone was born equal: she would grow indignant when I pointed out that the workings of nature were based on injustice. But I would not give in. I knew that she had been born a star, and set about trying to give her confidence in her natural gifts. Only after winning an Oscar for her performance in *Klute* did she admit that I had been instrumental in her development as an actress.

'It took me several years to understand what you were trying to tell me,' she said.

She didn't enjoy shooting *Barbarella*. She accepted the part because I was enthusiastic about the project, but she disliked the central character for her lack of principle, her shameless exploitation of her sexuality, and her irrelevance to contemporary social and political realities. In fact *Barbarella*, for all its extravagant fantasy, contains a good deal of ruthless satire on the problems of our times. But humour is not one of Jane's strong points, and she usually fails to grasp a point unless it is stated explicitly. Women's Lib showed through Barbarella's outer space make-up. Today she still looks back on the part as a detestable symbol of women's status in a society of male oppressors, but while she was shooting, her feelings were less pronounced, and I have very pleasant memories of this particular period.

Everything appeared to be for the best in the best of all possible worlds. We seemed to have a perfect physical and mental understanding. I loved her country and her family and friends, and I thought she liked France and my friends. We shared the same feeling of curiosity about people and things, and the same love of travel. Professionally, our different approaches were a source not of antagonism but of creativity.

The very thing that should have set the seal on our happiness in fact forced us apart. According to romantic tradition, a home and children are the life-blood of a marriage. For us they were the bone of contention, the worm in the bud, the spanner in the works, the fly in the ointment.

Jane had discovered a farmhouse near Houdan and – so she said at the time – had fallen in love with it. As I have said already, I can live quite happily in an attic, though I have no objection to luxury either. All our available capital was swallowed up in buying and then decorating and furnishing the farmhouse which was soon coming along well. Jane was efficiency itself, supervising the laying out of the garden and the interior décor. There was an enormous amount to be done. I have little talent for this kind of thing, and contented myself with making suggestions and objecting when I didn't like something. Jane showed the patience of a saint, and had things removed or altered to suit my tastes. I felt that she was satisfying a deeply felt need, that here was an uprooted American planting roots for herself, and that in fact she was playing the part of the ideal wife. She was showing less sense of reality than children who believe in the games they play but are not completely taken in by them. Jane took the game for the real thing. One day she was to wake up and come to detest her role as mistress of the house. My mistake was not in having tied her down to playing this character – I am on the whole against the concept of bourgeois marriage – but in not having realized in time that she was going against her own nature. I almost understood what was going on when she started to plant a wood in the garden.

'Why didn't you want to buy a house with a wood in the first place then?' I asked. The thought of a tree which had not grown naturally seemed barbarous to me.

'I'd never find a wood exactly like the one I want,' she said.

She gave orders to the servants, made interminable lists every morning (she had a mania for lists), entertained our friends, and still found time to go to dancing lessons three times a week, and to the flea market on Saturdays, as well as keeping the accounts and dealing with the bills. She looked after Nathalie and my son Christian when he came to stay with us. I was impressed, and didn't hide my admiration. But I was becoming terribly spoilt. I am really ashamed of it now. My only excuse is that I never wanted that kind of life, and never forced it on Jane. When she now tells journalists that I had turned her into a domestic slave, she overlooks this distinction, which is not without importance, in my view. But Jane is very down-to-earth: a fact is a fact. Nothing else matters.

On reading through what I have just written I feel that I may have portrayed Jane in a rather unkind light. She could also be sweet, sensuous and full of laughter. Her mystery lay in her contrasting moods: she was both aggressive and vulnerable, intolerant and desperately anxious to understand other people, open and reserved, charming and as hard as nails – sometimes all at the same time. She seemed to communicate with women more easily than with men, which is why she was thought, quite wrongly, to have lesbian tendencies.

She was glad to be expecting a child, and felt confident it would be a boy, though actually it was our little daughter Vanessa who was growing daily inside her. Then all of a sudden something changed. Jane became distant, her expression frozen. I put these signs of distress down to her condition, but there was a deeper and more serious reason. One day she said to me, almost spitefully:

'How can you love me and respect me when I'm nothing!'

At that moment I learnt something she had been trying to make me understand for some time. She was suffering from an affliction which, since I can find no other word in the dictionary to describe it, I shall call 'non-identity'.

She had the feeling that she did not exist as an individual personality, and that her character, her desires and her motives had to be created intellectually. Five years of psycho-analysis in the States had not solved the problem, and indeed may even have made it worse. Her reasoning was terrifyingly simple: I am nothing, and anyone who loves me is in love with a vacuum or with his own fantasy. Therefore, I cannot feel respect for a man who respects me, since he is simply deluding himself. If he can make such a mistake, he must be a fool.

It is easier to solve an equation with three unknown quantities than to find the answer to this kind of problem. At any rate, I never found it.

After Vanessa was born the situation got worse. Despite everything, Jane had been hoping for a miracle. One often hears people say (though I do not share this view myself) that a woman is only really complete when she becomes a mother, that bearing a child is her one true act of creation. Jane could see that giving life to someone else was a marvellous experience, an exhilarating adventure, but not the ultimate purpose of her existence. Vanessa was there to breathe, to cry, to laugh, but Jane had to live too.

As her career as an actress and her function as a mother were not enough for her, she started to look elsewhere for her identity. She has apparently found it in politics and in devoting herself heart and soul to her own notions of social justice. She told me recently that she had at last started to live. I should very much like to believe it.

It was not a home, a husband or a child that she wanted, but a cause she could throw herself into. Women, the blacks, the Indians, class injustice, Vietnam – fortunately for her, there are more than enough causes to choose from.

If I sound sarcastic, that's just my way of looking at the world. But don't be misled – I know as well as anyone that there's nothing more fulfilling for a man or woman than the discovery of a real purpose in life.

To be quite frank, I can't make up my mind whether it's more upsetting to lose one's wife to a guitar player or to a noble idea. In the former case one can laugh at oneself, which brings some relief. In the latter, one feels less jealous. The first instance makes me think of Aragon's poem, 'So many tears for a tune on the guitar . . .' The second makes me think of Karl Marx, and the immutable laws of history. Either way, the next few months or years were to be extremely unpleasant to live through.

The events of May 1968 helped to form Jane's political awareness.

We might have spent this time in the peace and quiet of the farmhouse, but one morning Fate decided to send me three people who were to upset my plans and perhaps unwittingly change the course of Jane's life. Jean-Michel Lacor (my assistant), Philippe Lefebvre and Jean Maillan wanted to reinvigorate the Film Technicians' Union by replacing the old guard from the CGT – the General Confederation of Labour – with a team that had a more modern approach. The Young Turks were afraid of arousing people's fears, and had come to ask me to put my name forward at the next general meeting, when fresh elections for the committee and presidency were to be held. I was generally well thought of for my straightforward attitude and for the part I had played in various disputes between technicians, non-technical staff and producers. Politically I was a liberal and had nothing to fear from Communism, but as I had never been a militant I would not be suspected of being biased in favour of any particular faction. If I were elected president the new team would be able to work with me, prepare its programme and take over the organization a few months later. Although I felt that the union had indeed become ossified by routine and that a change would be salutary, I wasn't keen on militant trade-union action. Laziness, not lack of political conviction, was the reason for my reservations, as I humbly admit. But the Young Turks produced a number of arguments in their effort to convince me, and in the end I accepted. I hoped I wouldn't be elected, and I was genuinely surprised to find myself made president of the Union of French Film Technicians by a virtually unanimous vote.

A week later the revolution broke out. At least some called it the revolution, while others referred to it as the festivities, or the carnival, or the circus; now one talks about the 'events' of May '68. Obviously there was a good deal of confusion in Paris that May, and equally obviously the newly appointed president of an important CGT union couldn't remain inactive. Jane, now five months pregnant, attended most of the union meetings, and I kept her posted about the rest. I had drawn up an analysis of the position which was approved by my colleagues in the French Communist Party, but rejected by the others. And the others were in the majority. I believed that the revolutionary outburst, like the action of a safety-valve, was more in the nature of a temporary skirmish than a full-scale battle, and that the Communist Party alone had sufficient political unity to bring the episode to its proper conclusion. I simply did not believe that the Party was prepared to seize state power. I saw two main reasons for this: first, that it wasn't ready; and second, that it would immediately be overwhelmed by uncontrollable forces if it attempted to launch a full-scale revolution. It wouldn't be able to withstand disorders on the Left, or the show of force on the Right. If it embarked on a revolutionary course of action it would almost inevitably condemn France to a Fascist or hyper-reactionary regime within a very short space of time. I was sufficiently convinced of the political wisdom and intelligence of the Communist Party to guess that after giving its backing to the outburst of popular feeling it would do all it could to prevent an armed confrontation which, in the context, could only help the forces of reaction.

My activities, therefore, were essentially pragmatic. I

made efforts, for one thing, to persuade the more extreme elements to allow two big American productions to go ahead in France instead of forcing them to move to new locations in Italy. Knowing the Americans as I did, I knew that they would never want to shoot in France again if they lost millions of dollars because of political instability, and that this would result in serious unemployment in the film industry. However, I also urged the union to take advantage of the film producers' panic and press for concrete benefits, such as a forty-eight hour week and two whole rest days a week.

Almost miraculously, and thanks to action by the workers at the Victorine studios in Nice, the first point was conceded. But otherwise things didn't go so well. I remember that at the end of a producers' meeting at Edmond Tenoudji's, I had managed to get the producers to agree to making the whole of Saturday a free day. This led to my being accused in the union of showing political naïvety and collusion with capitalists. The agreement was never ratified, de Gaulle returned, and a compulsory forty-eight hour week in the cinema industry had to wait two years.

All I learnt from these events was that people are disarmingly shameless when it comes to changing their allegiance – an unpleasant fact I hadn't had to face since the Occupation.

Jane, on the other hand, found much to reflect on. Her blue eyes, with their serious watchful look, were discovering a new world.

On 28 September my third child Vanessa was born.

In January we left again for California.

The beach at Malibu hadn't changed. It was still a happy place for us. And now in little Vanessa we had something extra – though, in the change that had come over Jane, we also had something less. But I continued to shut my eyes to the warning signs.

Jane was breast-feeding the baby. She still wore her

hair long, but she had to have it all cut short for the film about the dance marathons of the 1930s, *They Shoot Horses, Don't They*. Hers was a very exacting part. She often slept at the studios so as to keep her make-up on overnight. I used to go and see her there. She seemed possessed by fatigue and unhappiness – beautiful, pitiful and touching. She was living her part with an almost morbid intensity. A tenuous shadow, an indefinable sense of drifting apart, seemed to be falling between us like an icy barrier and I began to feel I was living a nightmare. The sensation was so fleeting that although I felt a stab of pain whenever we parted I was always able to convince myself that it was only an illusion. The erosion of love is sordid, shabby and absurd. A shaming and useless affliction. It is not even a lost battle, it is a cancer that eats away body, soul and mind. No one ever completely recovers from it.

But I am anticipating. At the time neither Jane nor I imagined that our marriage was in danger. The feeling of unease I have described only happened very occasionally.

At the beginning of July we left New York on the *France*. Andy Warhol had come to see us off before we sailed. I remember he was filling a sack with empty Coca-Cola bottles, like a miser who has come across a hoard of gold.

'Coca-Cola haven't been making embossed bottles for four years now,' he told me. 'It's getting hard to find them in the States.' He thought of the bottles as old masters, and was waiting avidly for the day when they would be worth a fortune.

We said goodbye to the Statue of Liberty from the bridge. I had the feeling that I was saying goodbye to something for ever. The five-day voyage was my last clear memory of happiness between us. After that everything becomes confused. My memory of unhappiness is never chronologically accurate.

Jane's trees were flourishing, and the garden was a mass of flowers. Vanessa took her first steps on the day of the first moon landing. During her dancing lessons Jane met a woman friend of hers who was travelling out to India, and decided to accompany her. She was going in search of herself. I stayed at Houdan with the baby.

When I received her long love letter from Nepal I realized that it was all over. She told me she loved me, that she would never allow life to separate us again. She needed me, and wanted to deserve our happiness.

It was touching and so full of good intentions that it sent a shiver down my spine. Between the lines I could read the intensity and sincerity of her desire to save our marriage, and her panic at not being sure that she would succeed. If she had still loved me she would have told me about the old Buddhist priest who had become a junkie, and the sunsets, and then asked me to get on the next plane and come out to join her.

For some reason which I am completely unable to explain, from the moment she returned we enjoyed a strange and intense physical understanding. Then, one day, it stopped abruptly. In a room in the Beverly Wiltshire Hotel in Hollywood she told me that we would have to separate.

She was very kind to me in the months following our separation – a good nurse. But cholera cannot be cured with cold compresses. If I had had the slightest tendencies towards suicide I should not be here now writing my memoirs, but luckily I have been blessed with admirable powers of recovery, and I managed to regain my enjoyment of living and loving. But it wasn't easy.

19. A charmed life

I was now living on my own once more. California was the highly coloured setting, permanently fascinating and sometimes dangerous, in which I was bringing up my two daughters. The beach was quiet enough on the whole, though one had some strange encounters.

One night, when the nanny was away, I had put Vanessa in my bed. I was woken up at dawn by the little girl, a strange noise, and found that she had got out of bed and was playing with the curtain. I was about to tell her to get back into bed when I saw two faces glued against the window. They were completely motionless, and in the cold, blue-green light of the dawn looked strangely unreal. The fixed, empty eyes with their unwavering stare reminded me of the sad-looking monsters in Goya's *Capricios*. Vanessa, who was not in the least afraid, was having fun playing hide-and-seek with them, drawing the curtains back and forth. The nightmare faces kept appearing and disappearing. Finally, a hand appeared on the window-frame and gave it a push which made the wood squeak.

I got up, grabbed hold of Vanessa, and ran off to put her in bed with my elder daughter Nathalie, who gave a little moan but mercifully didn't wake up. I locked their door from the outside and went into the living-room where the telephone was. Then, through the french window, I caught sight of the two men, watching me from the terrace. The horrible butchery of Roman Polanski's young wife, Sharon Tate, and her three friends had taken place only a mile or two away a month earlier. It was still fresh in my mind and every day the papers and television carried news of fresh crimes, all committed with the same insane, motiveless savagery. In almost every case chance alone had brought the murderers and their victims together.

I had to make a decision quickly. If I called the police the men would have ample time to break into the house and massacre us all. But what if they were merely drugged? In that case, even if the police did manage to arrest them, they would try to take their revenge later on. I had no firearms in the house – and if I had, it wouldn't have solved anything. I could hardly fire in cold blood at two men just because they happened to be standing on my terrace. And if I didn't fire, they might attack me first, either out of fear or because they felt provoked.

I walked unhurriedly towards the french window and opened it.

'Hallo there,' I said.

They made no move. I could see by their eyes that they were drugged, probably with a hallucinogen – LSD or mescaline. For them time wasn't passing at the same pace as it was for me. A minute for them might seem like an hour – or a fraction of a second. I waited. One sat down on the ground, with his back against the wall, while the other climbed on to a table. The one on the ground drew a revolver out of his pocket and rested it on his knee.

'Since you've woken me up,' I said, 'I'm going to make the most of it and go fishing. The tide's out and it's the right time for it.'

The important thing was to remain natural – above all not to show that I was afraid. But I couldn't be too familiar either, or they'd take offence. Under the effect of a hallucinogen the slightest movement, the most carefully concealed intentions are seen as if through a distorting lens and multiplied a thousandfold. I couldn't be sure about their ages, but I guessed they were between twenty and thirty-five.

'Yes,' said the one sitting down.

A minute later he repeated it: 'Yes.' He still had the revolver in his hand.

'I'm going to have something to drink,' I said. 'Are you thirsty?'

'Wine,' said the man with the revolver.

'Red,' said the one on the table.

I went into the house, took a bottle of Californian burgundy out of the fridge, grabbed three glasses, all in record time, and went back to the terrace, where I found the two men still in the same positions.

They seemed to trust me. But there was still that damned revolver, and the thing was by no means over yet.

The one sitting down accepted a glass, the other drank out of the bottle and then handed it back to me.

'Ronald Reagan is a shit,' said the one with the revolver.

'Yes, a dirty bastard,' I agreed.

I would have prostituted my own mother if it would have kept them happy.

'A flying turd,' said the man on the table.

The atmosphere was becoming less tense.

After five minutes' silence the one with the revolver suddenly burst out laughing and got to his feet. He walked off towards the sea and the other one followed him. I waited till they had disappeared from sight, behind the rocks to the north, then I went back into the house.

My first instinct was to call the police, but on reflection I decided against it. Even if they were given a short prison sentence for carrying firearms (though in America that isn't a crime in itself), they might try and take revenge when they got out. The best thing seemed to be to keep watch on the beach till the sun came up; if I saw them returning I'd have time to get the girls out of bed and drive to safety.

Six months later I saw pictures of the two men on a television programme. They'd killed three people in a car near San Francisco 'because the wife had complained that they smelled bad'.

After this interlude nothing really sensational troubled

our life on the beach – unless, of course, you count the earthquake and the big fire.

The earthquake was the biggest since the one in San Francisco in 1906. Two thousand dead and injured, whole blocks destroyed – it was quite a show, fully up to the standard of a Hollywood epic.

It happened during the night. I woke up with the queer impression that my bedroom walls were playing hop-scotch. Nathalie was screaming with fright in her room next door. I got out of bed and tried to go to her. It's easier to walk the wrong way up an escalator than it is to get to the other side of the room during an earthquake, and the noise made me lose my sense of balance quite as much as the actual shocks.

I clearly remember being in an earthquake in Turkey when I was six years old, and I know from books and from eyewitness accounts that earthquakes usually produce an irrational, overwhelming panic in both men and animals. So I don't really expect anyone to believe me when I say that in my case they produce exactly the opposite effect. Only my anxiety for the children spoilt my enjoyment. Finally I managed to get hold of Nathalie and push her out into the garden. Vanessa was laughing obliviously at the sight of her cot bouncing from one wall to the other – perhaps she had inherited some of her father's perverse pleasure. Dot, our old nanny, was taking it all with typical British coolness. Eventually all four of us found ourselves together in the garden, with the earth still moving beneath our feet. The first shock-wave lasted for over two minutes, which is a very long time indeed. Almost a record, it seems.

Nathalie was now going to the French *lycée* in Los Angeles, but that day and for the next few days she was excused class. She decided that, after all, natural disasters had some good points.

The fire was much more impressive.

I was at the MGM studios, shooting *Pretty Maids All*

in a Row, a black comedy set in a mixed high school. Towards the end of the afternoon I heard that a huge fire, fanned by a thirty-knot wind, was making its way down the hills towards the coast over a stretch of twenty miles and more. Malibu lay almost directly in its path. Army and police helicopters were evacuating people who hadn't been able to get away by road. Fortunately Vanessa was in New York with her mother, and as it was the school holidays Nathalie was with Annette Stroyberg and her new husband in the Bahamas. My first thought was for my 16mm films, particularly the ones I had taken of Vanessa since she was born. My idea was to put together a series of brief shots of all the most important moments of her life, and present her with a documentary of her development from new-born baby into a woman on her sixteenth birthday. Then I thought of the other Nathalie, my niece, who had come to spend a few weeks with me on the beach. At twenty she was old enough to look after herself, but all the same she hadn't got in touch with me and I was worried. Telephone communications with Malibu itself were cut, but the police assured me that there was nobody left in the area. By six o'clock, when shooting finished for the day, I still had no news from the older Nathalie. 'She's so scatter-brained,' I thought to myself, 'that she might have missed being picked up by helicopter.' The only thing to do was to go back to the house.

A cloud of black smoke, with the red glow from the fire reflected at its base, was pouring into the sky to a height of over three miles. There were road-blocks on the Pacific Coast Highway, and from the Santa Monica exit, ten miles or so from Malibu, three lanes of immobilized cars jammed the road.

As there was nobody coming in the opposite direction I moved over into the fourth lane, ignoring the other drivers' frantic signals. Some seven miles farther on there was a police barrier right across the highway. There was no question of being allowed through. The sun was still high in the sky, and yet it was almost as dark as night. I noticed that some fire-engines and army trucks were getting through the barrier, and this gave me an idea. I drove on to the hard shoulder and waited, with the engine running, for the next fire-engine to come along. I didn't have to wait long. The darkness was in my favour, and I managed to slip in between two fire-engines. I went through the barrier without taking my foot off the accelerator.

The fire-engines turned off the Highway farther up, and I continued alone.

Twice I found myself passing huge tongues of fire which were already almost licking the Highway. The heat was cruel, but I met with no other difficulties. Finally I reached Malibu. Here and there the fire had managed to break through as far as the houses on the beach, but then it seemed to have receded. At the moment, the leading edge of the fire zigzagged round the foot of the hills, about three hundred yards away.

I found my niece coughing and choking in the living-room. She didn't seem surprised to see me: she said she had been terrified at the idea of climbing into a helicopter and had hidden when the police had ordered everyone to leave the houses.

'I was sure you'd come and get me,' she said.

I thanked her for having so much trust in me, and we made up a bundle of things that I wanted to save (my films first of all).

I didn't dare attempt the return journey with a passenger. Even if I'd been on my own, I doubt whether I would have risked it a second time. I had a flat-bottomed boat which I used for fishing and kept on the beach, but when I got near the water I saw that there were gigantic waves breaking on the sand. It was out of the question to take the boat out in that sea – we'd have been flung back like a cork. We would just have to sit it out.

At the northern end of the beach about thirty houses

had already been destroyed. At the southern end two others were in flames, and the firemen were hard at work trying to contain the blaze which was being spread by flying debris. Our house was entirely covered with ivy, and was relatively protected, but ashes were getting in everywhere. The beach was the colour of solidified lava.

Nightfall made us cry out with amazement. I have never, in all my life, witnessed such a magnificent spectacle. The fire had now spread along a front of sixty miles and the whole range of mountains, as far as the eye could see, seemed to be going through a series of convulsions filmed in slow motion. Red and black shapes were locked together in a silent, voluptuous embrace. Close at hand the bright, shifting glow from the burning houses contributed a violent counterpoint to the majestic chords of the main orchestra. I had the feeling of listening with my eyes to a silent symphony.

Towards midnight the most beautiful of the houses along the beach, only two buildings away, caught fire. The firemen had succeeded in rescuing some valuable objects and furniture before the flames reached the lower storey, but they couldn't get the fire under control, and had to be content with playing their hoses on the houses next door. Three of them were clearing the garden of what they considered to be the most valuable possessions. Several pictures had escaped their attention and were lying on the grass. It was my niece who discovered them: two Picassos, a Modigliani, a Matisse and a Salvador Dali. I called out to one of the firemen and asked him to help us put these masterpieces somewhere safe.

'Are they worth something, then?' he asked suspiciously.

'Six or seven hundred thousand dollars,' I replied – whereupon he let rip a stream of swear-words on the lines of 'Well, I'm a son of a bitch, shit that, holy cow', and so on. One way of paying tribute to the masters, I suppose. I think Salvador Dali would have appreciated it.

The fire lasted for two days, but there was no further

damage down by the beach. Farther up in the hills, though, a lot of people were burnt alive.

At that time Hollywood was going through its death agony. The influence of the *nouvelle vogue* in France, and the restrictions imposed by the trade unions had dealt a fatal blow to the big film studios. The commercial success of films like *Easy Rider* and *Five Easy Pieces*, which were shot without stars and for a tenth of the budget of the traditional Hollywood productions, posed a serious threat to the existence of the American cinema. When I started shooting *Pretty Maids All in a Row* for MGM there was not a single other film under production in any of the six main Los Angeles studios. It was a strange paradox that the only director working in the legendary stronghold of the cinema should be a Frenchman.

The vast MGM studio complex looked like a ghost town in the Wild West. Three thousand people were still employed in the offices and workshops, but the legendary faces which had set the world dreaming were no more than shadows; the machinery continued to turn, but with no real purpose – like a train that keeps on moving even though the driver is dead. Whole truckloads of effects were sold at auction – Greta Garbo's dresses, Mae West's brassières, and Clark Gable's ties. The Wild West township and the Prohibition era street were slowly decaying from disuse, silence and rain. Takings from the sale of relics, furniture and costumes were supplemented by the daily flow of tourists who were taken round the dream factory like visitors to the ruins of Pompeii. Hollywood was living like an old Russian princess who has pawned the family jewels so that she can continue to keep a maid.

The ossification of the studios did not mean, however, that the cinema was completely dead. Hollywood preserved its heroes in a state of suspended animation, hoping that in time a remedy would be found for the disease. The big stars let the days go by in the seclusion of their gardens.

I used to meet them at premières, at Oscar presentations or with friends. Once Katharine Hepburn arrived at George Cukor's very put out because her basset hound didn't get on with the veterinary psychiatrist who was treating it. Another time Groucho Marx made the passengers in a lift laugh so much that they forgot to get out and it arrived at the top as crowded as the cabin in *A Night At The Opera*. Cary Grant would parade his charm and elegance at the races and one came away feeling that his grey hair was a sign of youth. And then there were all the others – Fred Astaire, Bing Crosby, James Stewart, Henry Fonda, Frank Sinatra, Dean Martin, Jennifer Jones, Lauren Bacall, Shirley Maclean, Marlon Brando, Paul Newman – who enabled the legend to live on in the present. I had a lot of friends among the more recent arrivals whose careers were less tied to the studios: Warren Beatty, Jack Nicholson, Peter Fonda, Mia Farrow, Faye Dunaway . . .

Today Hollywood has undergone a metamorphosis, and is being reborn from its ashes. I believe that the film I shot there was one of the last to be made in the old traditional way. It alone had three thousand MGM employees working on it: there was one department for supervising the script, another for casting, a third for the extras, a fourth for the sets, and so on *ad infinitum* for costumes, technical work, transportation, locations, administration, camera-work, publicity, sound, editing, etc., etc. Only in Russia have I seen such cancerous bureaucratic growth.

One day I needed to shoot a young boy on his motor-scooter from three different angles. In the morning a motorized column consisting of four trucks, the generating set, caravans for making up, actors, extras, the producer, the director, costumes and mobile kitchens, plus six or seven production cars set out from the studios. The drivers' union even refused to allow me to drive my own car. However, I managed to slip away unseen, accompanied by my director of photography, who had become a friend and accomplice. The actor followed on his motor-scooter. After an hour, using a shoulder-held camera, we had all the takes I needed. By the time the column arrived it was all over – and the studios had reckoned on two whole days of shooting!

I hated the idea of using a budget of three and a half million dollars for a film which shouldn't have cost more than eight hundred thousand, but even so, I found it an enthralling experience. The workers and technicians, actors, producers, and the president and vice-president of the corporation, all turned out to be very friendly and delighted to work with me. In fact it was the most enjoyable piece of film-making I have ever done in my career. In the States I never felt that sullen envy towards anyone who is successful which is so characteristic of France – in fact, if the Americans have a fault it is rather that they don't like losers.

Rock Hudson and Angie Dickinson led a brilliant cast which, because of the story, included a large number of young actors. Before I took them on I had auditioned over two hundred boys and about the same number of girls.

Most of the girls who applied were would-be actresses, though some were students who merely found the whole thing amusing. For a man convalescing from a love affair this cascade of young beauties should have been an excellent tonic. It wasn't unpleasant, of course, but I have never been a believer in sheer numbers. The heart has its own logic, which common sense knows nothing about. I was like a man washed up on a desert island who discovers, when he opens a newspaper that's been saved from the wreck, that he had made a fortune on the stock exchange. Good for morale, but of only limited interest in his predicament.

The film was entertaining, without being ambitious. The notices were fairly good in Los Angeles, dreadful in New York, and excellent in other towns. On the whole it was a success. I could have stayed on in the United States, where I had no lack of offers, but I decided to return to France.

A summer or two ago Vanessa (who was then five) and I were walking along the Chemin de la Citadelle which runs above the maritime cemetery at Saint-Tropez. She calls it the 'dead people village'. She was asking me questions about death and the survival of the soul. She thought on the whole that there was probably some kind of existence after death, but was afraid there might not be any sensible place where we could arrange to meet each other. Her face clouded over, and a few silent tears ran down her cheeks. Then, all of a sudden, her expression brightened.

'We shall just have to die at the same time,' she said.

It is a difficult promise to keep, but I gave my word I would live till I was very, very old so that I would wait for her. Then the conversation turned to the existence of God.

'I don't believe God exists,' she pronounced.

'Why not?'

'Mummy doesn't believe in God. But Grandma does. I know that the Son of God exists.'

'If the Son of God exists, then God must exist.'

She appreciated the logic of the argument, and thought for a moment.

'God is dead,' she said. 'And I know who He was. He was the first man.'

'You mean that God is the beginning of life?' I asked.

'He was the first man.'

We went on from there to talk about the Devil. She had difficulty in placing him, and asked me to explain. I told her the story of God and the angels, and how Satan had rebelled against the Creator and had been cast out of Heaven into Hell. I explained that though there were some people who believed in the story, I couldn't guarantee its authenticity. She found the story interesting, but not really very plausible. The concept of good and evil was still beyond her, though thanks to television she already knew the difference between goodies and baddies.

A few days later she started talking to me again about the Devil.

'I know why he was thrown out of Paradise,' she said.

'Why was he?'

'Because he didn't do things the way everybody else did.'

Index